Parenting Today's
Teenager Effectively

Hear Me
Hug Me
Trust Me

Parenting Today's
Teenager Effectively

Hear Me
Hug Me
Trust Me

Dr. G. Scott Wooding

Fitzhenry & Whiteside

Fitzhenry & Whiteside Edition – 2003
Text copyright © 1995 by Dr. G. Scott Wooding
Illustrations copyright © 1995 by Ron Leishman

1st published in 1995 by Script Publishing Inc.
Appendix updated in 2003

Published in Canada by Fitzhenry & Whiteside, 195 Allstate Parkway, Markham, Ontario L3R 4T8
Published in the United States by Fitzhenry & Whiteside, 121 Harvard Avenue, Suite 2,
Allston, Massachusetts 02134

www.fitzhenry.ca   godwit@fitzhenry.ca.

Fitzhenry & Whiteside acknowledges with thanks the Canada Council for the Arts,
the Government of Canada through the Book Publishing Industry Development Program (BPIDP), and
the Ontario Arts Council for their support of our publishing program.

Edited by Sherry Wilson McEwen
Design & page layout by Eileen Eckert
Illustrations by Ron Leishman
Cover Design by Kerry Designs

10 9 8 7 6 5 4 3 2 1

National Library of Canada Cataloguing in Publication
Wooding, G. Scott, (Gary Scott), 1944-
Parenting today's teenager effectively : hear me, hug me, trust me / by
G. Scott Wooding. — 2nd ed.

Includes index.
ISBN 1-55041-771-1

1. Parent and teenager. 2. Parenting. 3. Adolescence. 4. Adolescent
psychology. I. Title. II. Title: Hear me, hug me, trust me.

HQ799.15.W66 2003   306.874   C2002-905907-0

U.S. Cataloging-in-Publication Data
(Library of Congress Standards)

Wooding, G. Scott.
Hear me, hug me, trust me : parenting today's teenager effectively
/ G. Scott Wooding.
[224] p. : ill. ; cm.
Summary: Teenagers from their own unique perspective, offer the reader a 12-point definition of the
"ideal parent," and discuss what they like and dislike about the way their parents treat them.
ISBN 1-55041-771-1 (pbk.)
1. Parent and teenager. 2. Parenting. 3. Teenagers. I. Title.
649/.125 21   HQ799.15.W66 1995

CONTENTS

Out of the Mouths of Teens

❝ I myself have wonderful parents. But there are some kids who don't have good parents. I think that they need good or better parents because no matter how much our parents make us mad, we need them as a sense of security. We need to be loved. ❞
– Kristi

The idea for this book started with a Grade 9 classroom exercise in a subject called "Group Guidance." While discussing the need for rules, both at home and in school, several of my students complained about their parents and the unfair rules they were forced to live by. This led to an exchange on different methods of parenting, which rapidly deteriorated into a gripe session about parents in general. To regain control, I asked them to form groups of four or five and design the "Ideal Parents." To be honest, I expected the model parents to be a pair of adults who were generous with allowance money and relatively slack on rules. Instead, most of the groups came up with sets of characteristics that were as complete and realistic as any parenting expert could devise. After talking about their "designs," it became obvious that agreement could be reached on a set of universal parenting characteristics acceptable to most students. I repeated the exercise with four other Grade 9 classes, with almost identical results.

While the discussion was interesting, it may have remained a classroom exercise had not one of the students asked, "If we know this stuff, how come our parents don't?" A pertinent question. How to get this information across so that they would listen? Starting a dinner-table talk about what happened in school today would not work, for several reasons. A main reason was that the teens complained that their parents didn't listen to them, so there was no reason to believe this discussion would be different. Many families did not *have* dinner together, and finding their parents in the same location and in a receptive mood was very difficult for most of the students.

Eventually we decided to print the results of the classroom exercise and distribute them to parents of class members. A committee of volunteers was formed. The original idea was to produce a pamphlet for local distribution. But it became evident that listing characteristics would not be enough — most of the parenting traits required explanation. (For example, to say that parents should be "fair" is pretty vague, as most parents already think they are.) So the committee set about writing a book — deciding what topics should be included, and how the book should be organized.

The next stage, the writing, proved to be too much. The discipline involved was too much like homework, and writing about this topic was too difficult a job for ninth grade students. So the students collected data and the teacher wrote — and wrote —for over two years.

That is why this book is different. The difference lies in the fact that the information comes from the teens, and not from a theoretical expert in the field of family relationships. Even though they may not know much about the *theory* of parenting, teens know what they *like*. The fact that what they like turns out to be reasonable, and that it agrees with most parenting "experts," is more than a happy coincidence — it has resulted in a parenting manual that *will work* if the recommendations are followed and adapted to your own circumstances.

Hear Me, Hug Me, Trust Me is designed to be practical and easily read. It is based on the experiences of adolescents and their understanding of the world, with actual quotes from the teens who took part in my classroom surveys (the names have all been changed, to protect their privacy and that of their parents).

While not intended to be scientific, the sample of teens is representative of the majority of teenagers in Canada and the United States. The sample consists of hundreds of students from ages 12 to 16, from a wide variety of cultural and economic backgrounds. They represent a large cross-section of typical teens.

Hear Me, Hug Me, Trust Me focuses on the teens themselves and what they have to say about parenting. As a professional whose life work has been dealing with teens in the role of psychologist, counselor and teacher, my goal has been to pull this information together, and to add my experience where necessary. Teachers know that you can't fool the kids. Teens know who's a good teacher and who the bad ones are. As you'll see in this book, the same goes for parents. You can't fool the kids!

HOW THIS BOOK IS ORGANIZED

In Part A of the Introduction, "Meet the Modern Teen," we analyze today's adolescent — the way they really are, rather than the way they would like to be. In Part B of the Introduction, "The (Almost) Ideal Parent," I have listed the characteristics that most teens want their parents to have. There are 12 of these characteristics, and they form the first 12 chapters of the book. This is followed by a summary of the "Hear Me, Hug Me, Trust Me" approach to parenting. Then I add my experience to the teens' characteristics with a "troubleshooting" chapter, where solutions to some of the most common teenage problems are discussed. Finally, since no one book can cover everything about this incredibly complex topic, I have added an appendix of other works about teens.

This book is designed both as an overall system of parenting, for those with young teens, and as a "solutions" book, for parents who are well into the process, but could use some advice in specific areas.

“ I like my parents a lot because they state fair and reasonable rules and then outside that, I've got all the freedom I want. They let me make my own decisions, and they trust me to make reasonable ones. I know what is right and wrong for me and what I want, but if I ever need anything (support, to talk), they're there. ”
– *Sarah*

A. Meet the Modern Teen

❝ I hate when parents say 'When I was your age...' They never really were our age. They grew up in a very different time. Thus, I believe they shouldn't deal with us the same way their parents dealt with them. It's different now; they should see that but they don't. ❞
– Jennie

Is Jennie right? Is each generation completely different than any before? If today's teens are so different from their parents, the knowledge that the older generation gained from their own experiences growing up will not apply to their own children; if the teenagers of today are, in fact, similar to their parents, recalling your own feelings and behaviors will be helpful in raising your adolescent. The answer to the question appears to be a definite "yes" — and "no." Allow me to explain.

TEENS HAVE MORE KNOWLEDGE

Now don't get excited. I'm not saying they're smarter. Teenagers today simply have access to more facts on more subjects than did their parents (that's you). This is partly due to the evolution of communication. Satellite links between countries make information about

customs and lifestyles more accessible, even if the teens are only watching the news breaks between episodes of their favorite sitcom.

Another source of worldly knowledge comes from traveling, which
is much cheaper and more common now. Parents pride themselves
on being able to take their kids to exotic locations and schools run
visits to all parts of the world during holidays. This results in a more
sophisticated adolescent.

One area of knowledge where teens are significantly farther ahead
than their parents were when they were young is the subject of sex.
The sexual revolution of the late 1950s and the 1960s resulted in such
an explosion of information and misinformation that many school
systems were forced to include sex education in their curricula. This
ensures not only a broader knowledge of the subject, but a more factual one.

I remember being in Grade 7 (in 1956) when Oliver Robinow
dropped the bombshell about how babies were made, which he had

just heard from Michael Pooley. As you can imagine, there were several details missing. When I heard my mother mention "natural child-birth" a few weeks later, I assumed that this meant that babies could occur naturally, as opposed to the "unnatural method" which involved intercourse. This misconception was not straightened out for several years, until after the "chance" discovery of a copy of *Sex, Marriage, and Birth Control* (in Dad's top drawer). That was the "old way."

The extra factual knowledge teens have does not mean that they handle sexual encounters any better than their parents did, or that they know everything about the subject. It just means that they have more, and more accurate, information about sex at their disposal.

Other factors affecting the increased knowledge levels of today's teenager include computers, especially since the development of the CD-ROM, and the easy access to movies, including those on "adult" topics, through the advent of videotapes and VCRs. This knowledge explosion can tend to make teens overconfident about their ability to handle things like alcohol, drugs, and sex as they do not realize the power of emotions and peer pressure.

TEENS' LIVES ARE BUSIER AND MORE COMPLEX

This statement does not apply only to teens; the problem starts at an earlier age and results from a complicated series of changes in our society over the last 30 years or so. One cause is the relative affluence of parents over this period — they can afford to pay for more lessons and equipment for their children. Along with this affluence comes a parental philosophy, which has probably been present throughout history, of wanting more for their kids than they had themselves. Occasionally this attitude is born of parents building their own self-images on the success of their children. In any case, the result is a tremendous increase in the activities in which youngsters are enrolled. These activities are mainly in the areas of culture and sports, but also include extra academic opportunities. More children than ever before are registered in music lessons, dance classes, and organized sports. For students who show promise in school, there are university summer schools, and extracurricular enrichment classes. Good and even mediocre athletes attend summer basketball and hockey schools or soccer camps, or play in baseball leagues with seasons almost as long as those of the big leagues. Individually, none of these activities is a problem. In fact, unless the child absolutely hates it and is only doing it because of the parent, most activities are beneficial. But the situation becomes more difficult with each added endeavor. Many kids have at least one activity every night of the week. The result is busy young children who eventually become busy young adults.

This increased activity level is made more complicated because cities are bigger and faster-paced than ever. As families move further out into the suburbs, travel times through the traffic-snarled streets become longer. More children take school buses now, as inner city schools become empty. This means that kids have to get up earlier, and come home later. At the same time they are exposed to more noise, pollution and commotion than most parents experienced as children. The potential result is children who are much more tense than their parents were at the same age.

Increased activity levels combined with these urban realities result in some very uptight young people. When an argument begins, the explosion from the child is sometimes fiercer due to this added tension. As young people reach adolescence, when the desire for independence and a separate identity conflict with household rules and values, the resulting battles can be far out of proportion to the cause. Add to this the emotional state of the parents, who themselves are often physically and mentally exhausted, and the argument becomes far worse than it should be. Often the teens appear more defiant than they really intend. This — *the stress of modern living* — is the major difference between the modern teen and those of previous generations.

ATYPICAL FAMILIES MAKE TEEN LIVES MORE DIFFICULT

Another contributor to the tension levels of today's teen is the prevalence of atypical families. Over the last decade or so, there has been a tremendous increase in the number of single parents, stepparents and blended families. Each of these situations brings with it unique problems which add to those experienced in the normal course of being a teenager.

The difficulties experienced by teens with single parents include anger at both parents for "destroying" their family; wanting to live with the "other" parent as a result of the "grass is greener" effect; and the problem of interacting with a parent trying to earn a living and raise a family alone.

Teens with stepparents resent a stranger taking the place of a loved parent. This gets complicated by a stepparent who is unprepared for this reaction, and who responds defensively to the rejection. There are also problems with stepparents who try too hard to win over the teens, and with estranged natural parents who pour oil on the fires of resentment that already exist.

Blended families, where the stepparent brings his or her kids into the relationship, add to tensions by the differential treatment often accorded to "my" children as opposed to "yours." If "our" children appear, the formula becomes even more complex.

These are only a sample of the problems that teens in atypical families are likely to experience. They do illustrate the extra burden that teens in these situations may have to carry, and which add to the tension levels of today's teenager. While these special situations are rarely mentioned specifically in this book, the principles outlined in the subsequent chapters work as well with atypical families as they do with two-parent ones. In fact, they may be even more necessary and useful in these situations.

TEENS HAVE NOT CHANGED EMOTIONALLY

This is the crucial issue of this book: while teens may be more knowledgeable, and often more physically and emotionally tense, their emotional needs and control valves are no different than were their parents' at an equivalent age. Their factual knowledge of sex, for example, will not necessarily save them from having unprotected intercourse. Teens' emotions always override their reasoning powers, despite their knowledge of birth control and sexually-transmitted diseases. In this way they are the same as they have always been.

Similarly, knowledge of world affairs, social issues and geography do not lessen the effects of peer pressure, nor do they eliminate the need for security and communication. What this knowledge does do is give the *impression* that teens are more mature than they really are. The facts they have absorbed in school, in their travels, and from television make them seem capable of handling circumstances more complex than could their parents. WRONG. The social situations confronting today's teens are as baffling to them as they were to their parents. This generation of teens make the same types of mistakes as did previous generations.

What does this mean for parents now? It means that the emotional issues that had to be confronted 25 years or so ago are still being encountered today. Parents' past experiences are therefore still relevant. The pain of being "dumped" by a boyfriend or girlfriend is as hard to take now as it ever was. Only the clothes have changed.

Speaking of clothes, it is just as important to wear the right ones now as it was — way back then. Peer pressure is just as strong, and today's teens have as much difficulty recognizing this fact as you did.

So Jennie is only partially right. (Chapter 2 will help you understand today's teen, so that your kids can't upset you with statements like Jennie's). The modern teen is different in knowledge and in the pace of life, and of course the styles and trends are different. These differences require that parents make certain adjustments in their thinking. For example, you can discuss topics today that would never have been talked about at home in previous years. But emotionally, teens have not changed from previous generations. They still need their parents at least as much as they did in the past, and possibly more.

WHO IS IN CONTROL?

"Who is in control?" is a primary theme that needs to be clearly stated right from the start. The major difference between adults and adolescents (other than age) is the ability of grown-ups to use their knowledge and experience to react logically to emotional situations. It's called "maturity." Since parents are (usually) adults, it follows that parents are (usually) more mature. Loosely, in philosophy this would be called a "syllogism."

The difficulty arises when arguments occur between teens and their parents. Since the teens are immature, and therefore not usually capable of mastering their emotions, it is the parent who must control the situation by staying calm. This gets extremely difficult if the parents are being screamed at, called names and told that they are rotten. The natural tendency is to react in kind. If this happens, the issue at hand will not only remain unresolved, but poor decisions will be made. No one is satisfied by the outcome and tension will rule the household.

> *It is the parent's responsibility to stay calm.*

The trick lies in staying calm and using that adult maturity to try to resolve the situation, preferably by some sort of compromise. Even if no compromise is possible, nothing is gained when both sides lose their tempers. It is the parent's responsibility to stay calm. The teen can be expected to become emotional; it's practically part of the definition of "teenager." This only leaves those on the other side of the argument to keep the situation in check.

When it looks like an argument is starting, involved parents need to ask themselves "Who's in control?" Keep the situation in perspective. If the answer is "I should be," the course is clear. Stay cool. This principle is so crucial to the spirit of this book that it needed to be said at the start.

B. The (Almost) Ideal Parent

In the preface I mentioned the fact that you can't fool teens. As the consumers of parenting, teens are in the best position to know how they like to be treated — even if they don't have any idea why they want to be treated in these ways.

The information in this book was collected over a period of four years. Teenagers were asked, either singly or in groups, to write down what they considered to be the characteristics of an ideal parent. Very few frivolous responses were turned in, and a pattern of characteristics quickly developed. Teen after teen wrote variations of the same points.

After analyzing the results of hundreds of these surveys, here is a brief summary of what the teens believe to be the twelve most important characteristics of an ideal parent.

TWELVE SUGGESTIONS TO PARENTS FROM TEENAGERS

1. Develop more UNDERSTANDING

Understanding involves listening to the teen's side of an issue and then having some empathy or feeling for why they feel the way they do. It also involves having some knowledge of key teen concerns such as peer pressure, their passion for loud music, their strange tastes in clothing, and the importance of their friends.

This understanding is not necessarily agreement — it only means that you can relate to what they are saying. You can disagree with them and still show that you understand and accept them.

2. Improve COMMUNICATION

Communication is a vital tool in developing a strong relationship with your teen. Two aspects are important — *listening* and *talking*. In being a good listener, you may have to hear some pretty shocking things without reacting to them visibly. Developing this skill requires time and patience. When a teen discovers that he or she can talk about virtually any topic without the parent constantly interrupting, judging, or expressing anger or disgust, the teen will be more willing to include the parent in all that is going on in her life.

When it comes to talking, teens ask for two things: (1) that the parents not yell, and (2) that they not lecture. By being calm and brief, parents can help to avoid conflict and to de-escalate emotional situations.

3. Provide appropriate DISCIPLINE

Surprisingly, most teens indicated that they want their parents to be "firm but fair" or "strict but not too strict." While they want and need some freedom to try things their way, this freedom can sometimes be scary. They want rules to provide a safety net for them to fall back on, when the freedom gets to be too much to handle. Limits provide this security for teens. Rules also show that parents care about them, an area where teens need constant reassurance.

Teens recognize the need for discipline, and they don't even mind taking the consequences if they know they've broken a rule. They just want the system to be fair. The guidelines for setting these rules include: (1) set a few *clear* rules; (2) allow the teens some input into these rules, and the consequences for breaking them; and (3) keep anger out of disciplinary situations.

4. Show FAIRNESS

Teens have a keen sense of justice. They want to be treated as individuals, not just members of a group. To teens fairness includes: (1) having their side of the story listened to in all circumstances; (2) being treated equally with regard to siblings; (3) being seen as an individual when it comes to abilities, such as intelligence or athletic talent; and (4) parents being consistent in their treatment of the

> **They just want the system to be fair.**

teens. Fairness in how chores are divided within the family, how rules are set for each sibling, and in how consequences for infractions of the rules are handed out can help to maintain positive relationships between parents and their teens.

5. Demonstrate TRUST

Trust is difficult for many parents because it involves taking chances. Teens want you to trust them first, before they have to prove themselves. They hate being checked on, and they want to be able to make some decisions for themselves. Trust is closely related to the independence teens need to establish their own identity. Unfortunately it is the parents who must sit at home and worry that all is going well at the party or downtown in the mall.

Showing trust in your teen involves not asking too many questions when he goes out, allowing her to make decisions, and believing explanations when things go awry. It requires a combination of courage to let them try some new things and faith in the fact that you as parents have done a good job in instilling the right values for your family. This is frightening for most parents, but rewarding when a trustworthy teen emerges.

6. Give RESPECT more freely

Another part of the teen need to establish a separate identity is the desire to be treated in a more adult fashion. They don't want to be treated exactly like adults — they're not ready for that — but they want more *respect* for their ideas, dreams, plans, and decisions. They want to think for and express themselves, without being put down, no matter how unrealistic these thoughts might be. They want support, not necessarily approval. They want to be asked their opinion, and to be given advice more gently and subtly than in the past.

7. Help develop RESPONSIBILITY

Teens want to develop into responsible people because they know that this leads to greater freedom, and it makes them feel like contributing members of the family — a more adult feeling. They recognize that responsibility is a quality of adulthood (the condition that they are trying to reach by next week). They know the only way they can do this is to be given tasks and duties that will build and require responsibility.

Teens actually want the responsibility of household chores. They need an allowance to learn how to handle money. And they have homework to prove their academic responsility. Unfortunately, because they are still teens, the chores, allowance and homework need parental follow-up to ensure that responsibility is being shown. This can require tremendous parental energy. Through a system of rewards and consequences and parental patience and persistence, a responsible teen will result.

8. Show signs of CARING

Teens want clear signs that you love and care for them. They want to *hear* the words "I love you" or "You're great to have around." They also need occasional physical signs of affection, like a hug or a squeeze; to be taken places they love to go; and even to have their parents worry about them. It doesn't take much, but it's needed. When they're in trouble they want you to support and comfort them first, before assessing blame. Teens need frequent reassurance that their parents will support them through thick and thin, even if later they have to accept the consequences for their part in the problem.

9. Demonstrate HONESTY

Teens want their parents to tell them when there are problems in the family, to be open in discussing "hot" topics such as sex and drugs, and to admit their errors on the rare occasions when parents are wrong. They crave this honesty because: (1) it help teens to trust their parents, which in turn makes them easier to confide in; (2) it helps them to understand parental decisions, like why they can't stay out till 2:00 a.m.; and (3) it sets a good example for them to follow. They can usually tell when parents are not telling them the whole story or when the truth is being "bent" a little, and they resent it. While it is often difficult to know how much truth a teen can handle, it is better to err on the side of honesty than to withhold the facts.

10. Display a sense of HUMOR

Don't be intimidated; teens don't expect stand-up comedy. What they yearn for is the occasional injection of humor into a difficult situation. Taking a situation seriously enough without taking it too seriously is a fine line, but some lightening up at the right time can get you both out of a tough spot. Timing is the key — for comedians and for parents. If your daughter has been dumped by her boyfriend, first listen sympathetically, then when self-pity begins to set in, gentle jokes about boyfriends and relationships may take some of the sting out of the problem.

Humor also makes authority easier to take, and is useful in seeing that household chores get done. Some can't make jokes on demand, but most of us have a sense of humor which can help to make home a more comfortable place for teens and parents alike.

11. Spend more TIME TOGETHER

As society has changed, parents have become more scarce at home. The phrase "quality time" was probably invented by a guilty parent.

> **There is no such thing as "quality time," there is only time with your kids!**

There is no such thing as quality time, there is only time with your kids. Teens typically think that parents work too much. Not only is time short, but so is patience. Minor mistakes by children become major issues to tired parents. While it is possible to go too far in spending time with your teens, most parents fall into the "too little" category. Parents should go to their kids' activities, take them on planned outings, have family nights, and even drop everything when the teen suggests a spontaneous activity. Even more important is to take the time to listen to them when they're down and need your sympathetic ear.

12. Set the EXAMPLE

Teens want to be able to look up to their parents, as role models for them to follow. When parents fail to live up to these expectations, they lose the respect of their teens and, worse, their credibility when they try to set rules. Teens hate to see their parents setting a bad example in the areas of arguing, smoking and drinking, yelling and losing their temper, and swearing. Teens believe that if an action is important enough to require a rule, it's important enough for parents to follow too. It's like parents expecting the government to follow the laws it passes.

Getting It All Together

There they are. Twelve characteristics that teens believe make up the "ideal" parent. Interestingly, most parenting "experts" would agree with the teens — and so does the research. If you are now feeling inadequate, don't panic. Nobody can be all of these things all of the time — that would take a saint. There are, however, ways to improve on the methods you may be using, usually out of instinct or habit rather than from a plan. Read on, practice the techniques a little, discuss them with your spouse, practice some more, and soon your teens will wonder what's been going right. Better still, they'll like it.

The Hear Me, Hug Me, Trust Me Approach

While it is important to understand the 12 characteristics that make an ideal parent, it can get very confusing. The list of "do's" and "don'ts" may seem so long that it becomes impossible to remember everything. For parents who care about their teens it really isn't that difficult. I've boiled the 12 steps down into one expression: "Hear me, hug me, trust me — and don't yell at me." The "Hear me, hug me, trust me" approach to effective parenting stresses listening to teens, even in disciplinary situations; showing them that you love them, even when they mess up; giving them freedom to try new things; and not yelling at them. You can be a great parent by understanding and following the "Hear me, hug me, trust me" approach. The 12 steps I discuss throughout this book expand on that theme and will help you develop a deeper understanding of teens and parenting. For more details on the "Hear me, hug me, trust me" approach, please see Chapter 13.

THE BIG TWELVE

- UNDERSTANDING
- COMMUNICATION
- DISCIPLINE
- FAIRNESS
- TRUST
- RESPECT
- RESPONSIBILITY
- CARING
- HONESTY
- HUMOR
- SPENDING TIME TOGETHER
- SETTING THE EXAMPLE

Teens: The Road Map

**((What definitely would help would
be if parents were more in tune
with what it's like to be a teenager.
Most parents nowadays have forgotten
what it was like when they were younger.))**
– Franklin

1. Develop more UNDERSTANDING

You say teenagers are just children who have grown older? Most teens would say, "No way!" or "Not!" or whatever expression is current — and they're right.

Psychologists and educators have spent thousands of hours trying to explain teenage behavior. What they have found is that rebellion and the search for a separate identity are part of maturing.

Why this is so isn't as important as what is normal behavior for a teen. **Many problems between parents and teenage children begin with lack of understanding.** There is a common tendency for parents to overreact to an issue when they don't realize that their teen's behavior is standard for the age group. It is important to be able to separate the common concerns from the real problems, in order not to "overparent." Concerns over messy bedrooms and too much time on the telephone tend to fade when you realize that most teens are like this. Understanding that the behavior is normal doesn't mean you have to tolerate it, it just means you don't have to worry about your "problem teen." It also means you can deal with typical situations much more coolly than you might with more serious concerns such as alcohol abuse and criminal activities.

Let's look at how you go about finding out what the average teen really is like.

PARENTAL RESEARCH

Remember When?

To empathize with your teen, spend some time thinking about your own hormonal imbalances and excruciating peer pressure. There is a selective form of amnesia that attacks parents just after they start a family, which erases most memories between the ages of 13 to 19.

Picture the clothes you wore. How did your folks feel about them? What type of music did you listen to? At what volumes? What were your major arguments about? How important were friends, privacy and junk food? Sit down and see how much you can remember. This trip into nostalgia could even be fun.

While at first you may not recall much, keep at it. You'll find you remember more than you thought possible. As a memory jogger, haul out your old yearbooks and call high school friends to ask about things that won't come back. Don't pick and choose; the purpose is to understand your own teen by re-examining all of your actions at a similar age. It helps to discover that there are inevitable similarities.

Talking with Other Parents

Many parents of teenagers seem to live in a vacuum when it comes to raising their children. Most don't network with other parents — if they did, they could find out that their teen is not the only one having problems. Ask other parents if their kid hates to take the garbage out or whines and complains when it's time to practice the piano.

These opportunities occur frequently, although parents often don't see their chance. There sometimes appears to be an unwritten law at social events, especially among fathers, that children will not be discussed. Parent-teacher nights, community events and sporting events are all good resources for a little modern anthropology.

If you are puzzled or concerned about certain teen customs, why not ask other parents if they see their young adults doing similar things? You will be amazed at how often they are! Even if the other parent is not having the same difficulties, don't stop there. Continue asking, until you either find that you aren't encountering a problem, but rather a common behavior among teens; or that you do have a unique situation. Either way you are further ahead than when you had no basis for comparison.

Modern Anthropology

> **Why not spend a few hours observing teens in the mall?**

Is wearing torn blue jeans unusual or *de rigueur*? Does every kid go out in the dead of winter wearing only tennis shoes? A valuable source of information about these and other puzzling adolescent practices is available in those massive teen entertainment centers called malls. Rather than hurrying through a shopping trip to escape the crowds, why not spend a few hours observing the local wildlife after school hours or on weekends? Linger over a cup of coffee in the food fairs and observe the kids' clothing and hairstyles. Sit at a table close to a group of teens and eavesdrop on the conversation. Drop into an arcade and peruse the video games, watch the teens who inhabit these places, and even listen to the music playing in the background. (More musical knowledge can be gained from checking out the displays in the record stores, and watching which tapes and CDs the kids are buying.) Why bother with all of this? Because it will allow you, the parent, to determine just where your teen fits in the adolescent world.

Taxi Service

Most mothers can identify with the bumper stickers that read "Mom's Taxi." In fact both parents often get to play taxi driver. Those who only chauffeur their offspring are missing a valuable source of current information about the species. Whenever possible, take a group of four or five kids to an athletic event, a concert, or to the mall. On the way there, remain quiet. After a few minutes they forget there's an adult in the car and start to talk about the most fascinating subjects.

The trick to learning about which teachers are the best, who is going out with whom, and where the party is next weekend is: *keep quiet. As long as the "taxi driver" can keep in character, the kids will keep talking.* Even though the language may occasionally get a bit raunchy, and some of the anecdotes may describe illegal and/or dangerous escapades, beware — a sudden exclamation of surprise or outrage will cause the information source to dry up.

This does not mean you can't talk about these topics later on, or that you should approve of the language or behavior described. It does mean: no negative reactions at the time. The kids will even answer questions if you seem truly interested, as long as you maintain a friendly tone.

Teen Talk

One of the best sources of information about teen customs is teens themselves. When their friends come over to the house, why not ask them about what chores they have to do around the house, or what their curfew is? Since teens generally choose their friends on the basis of common interests, what they like, your child will like. Use some of your mall research knowledge to ask questions, such as "What type of music do the 'Dead Pickles' play?" The kids will be more than happy to fill in an adult on the latest rock groups, if you show genuine interest. They'll be so amazed that an adult is interested in anything but easy listening music that you may get a dissertation on the subject.

Caution: ask only one or two questions at a time, to avoid sounding like an interrogator. Just a few questions per visit should be enough to build up a picture of the behaviors you want to know about.

DANGER AREAS

"Turn that down!" Consider the reaction three little words can evoke. You can almost guarantee an argument. "Are you really going to wear that?" usually gets a comparable response. The testy replies result from the teen's sensitivity about their taste, which is apparently being criticized. Knowledge of what issues are important to teens, plus a little foresight and creativity, can prevent considerable conflict over the years.

Music

Look out for this one! It's a "can't win" area. Music is vital to teens for reasons researchers are still discussing. Given this jewel of wisdom, what does it mean for parents? Craig, a teen, sheds some light on this question:

"Music is what gives everyone their own personality."

In other words, when you criticize the *music*, you criticize the *person*. Their identities are tied to the music they listen to. And it helps set them apart from you. When you don't like the music, it is very hard to listen to, especially at the volume kids insist on. Watching music videos can be a shock. The temptation to comment derogatorily is overwhelming. The resulting defensive reaction from the teens leads to arguments and a widening of the "generation gap."

Any effort to eliminate the offending music from your house or car or to influence the type of music your teen listens to will only result in arguments and eventually in the music going underground. You can't stop the kids from listening to what they, for whatever obscure reasons, like to hear — so there's no point wasting your energy and impairing your communications with them.

Let's examine the influence of music on teen behavior. Does "heavy metal" music, for example, cause adolescents to be wilder than they would normally be? This is a "chicken and egg" problem: does the teen's personality determine the type of music, or does the music cause the behavior? Teens favor the first explanation and I tend to agree with them. The more rebellious the teen, the more outrageous their music will be. The rebellion, however, comes first. The music is a clue to the personality, and can sometimes be a *symptom* of serious emotional problems. It is not the cause of them. *Don't blame the music —* the causes lie deeper.

Music will not cause a change in your teen's behavior. If there is a sudden radical change in the type of music your teen is addicted to, then either the kid has changed or perhaps his or her friends have changed. It can even be both.

Changing friends is common as adolescent hormones kick in. Often the new friends like a different type of music and, in order to fit in, your child will adopt it. This does not mean that the child is a mere pawn. The teen really believes he likes the music for its own sake and totally rejects the idea of peer pressure.

Does all this mean that you are condemned to having your house and car throbbing to the beat throughout your teen's waking hours? Of course not. It's still your house and car, and you have the right to impose limitations. It's reasonable to reserve the household stereo when you are at home. Earphones and portable tape and CD players are inventions from heaven — insist that your teens use them in their own rooms. The trick is to impose these restrictions with understanding and, as far as possible, without making judgments. If you can do this then teens, music and parents can co-exist quite nicely. (There will be more on the "how to" side of this in the next chapter.)

Clothing

Consider these two brief scenarios, and see if they sound familiar:

Mother:	"Where's that pretty red sweater I bought you last Christmas?"
Daughter:	"I don't know."
Mother:	"Well why don't you know? It looks great on you and it cost a fortune."
Daughter:	"I look like a geek in it, so I never wear it. It's probably in my closet somewhere."
Mother:	"What do you mean you look like a geek in it? You liked it when I bought it. You were right there with me."
Daughter:	"Well I changed my mind. O.K.?"
Mother:	"No it's not O.K.. Have you any idea what it cost? Money doesn't grow on trees, you know."

... and the argument escalates from there.

Father: "You're not wearing those running shoes to school are you? It's 40 below out there."

Son: "It's not that cold, I'll be fine."

Father: "I know how cold it is, and you will not be fine if you wear those shoes. Get your boots on."

Son: "Da-a-ad! My feet never get cold. I don't need those dumb boots."

Father: "Either you put your boots on or you don't go to school. Take your choice."

Son: "That's not fair - you're always telling me how I should dress. I'm old enough to know whether I'm cold or not."

... and the argument escalates from there.

If you have not run into situations similar to these, you soon will. While the subject of clothing is as important to most teens as is their music, the tastes of parents and teens differ just as widely. Why is clothing so important? It probably starts with teenagers wanting to establish an identity different from their family. Kari says, "Teens want to be like their friends or want to be noticed by other people of the same or opposite sex."

The elements of individuality and peer pressure, found in the teenage need for different music, are again present. But this time they are complicated by the need to be attractive to the opposite sex. This makes the issue even more potentially explosive.

Take the first scenario. The daughter may have liked the sweater when she saw it in the store, but later found that no one else in her peer group had one. Or perhaps some boy she liked said something negative about it. It doesn't take much for teen clothing to be relegated to the back of the closet forever.

In the second situation, the problem is again one of what others in the peer group wear. Only those not "with it" wear overshoes to school at the adolescent level, no matter what the temperature! There is also some truth to the son's statement that his feet never get cold. Teens often do not feel the cold as much as an adult does. The reason for what most parents would describe as "No sense, no feeling" is probably more to do with attitude than with physiology. When with friends, teens are so preoccupied with adolescent issues that they don't notice the cold as adults do.

What are some other clashes over clothing that teens identify? One is labels. A pair of blue jeans with the "right" label often costs twice as much as a similar pair of generic jeans. This baffles parents, but is perfectly clear to their young ones, who can spot the real thing at 500 yards. In some groups there is status conferred by having the right label. Teens are openly admired by their friends and covertly by other peers for wearing the "in" label. This makes them feel better about themselves and, as teens, anything that helps to make them feel more secure is good. As Mike clearly states:

"The most important thing in my life right now is my social life. Trying to fit in is so important and believe me I try to get the right clothes and act right."

As most teenagers do not have a well developed sense of responsibility about money, practical considerations don't count. They can't really explain why, they just know they like the "labels" better.

Another touchy clothing-related issue is their care. Since the hippie era of the late 1960s and early 1970s, the trend has been toward casual, even downright sloppy clothing. Most parents are baffled as to why a teen would rip the knees out of a perfectly good pair of jeans (label or no label), or write all over their new running shoes. When asked, teens can't really explain either, except to say "it's cool." Again, it's a question of fitting in with the group. Neat, well-pressed clothes are for the unpopular kids.

Where do these styles come from? The kids think what they wear is their idea, and argue vehemently they aren't being influenced by anyone else. Adults know differently, but there's not much point in pointing this out. In fact, the styles are set by rock groups, popular teen idols and clothing designers and manufacturers. Shhh! Don't tell the teens.

Like music, this does not mean that parents should let their kids wear whatever they want. Kari's advice to parents is, "Keep an open mind and be flexible — bend a little." This is probably the best approach. Kids would rather fight you than their friends, so give a little. Periodically check what the current fashions are (they change quickly). Decide what your limits are. If your teen does not get colds from going out in running shoes and an open spring jacket in the winter, why worry about it? If your daughter's treatment of her clothes wears them out too quickly, then discuss this issue calmly but firmly with her. One possible solution is have her buy her own clothes, or a percentage of them, out of her allowance or babysitting money. If your son has a habit of not wearing good clothing shortly after you buy it, then he too should pay for all or part of the cost of the clothes. If the teens have a financial stake in their clothing, they will tend to choose it more carefully and look after it better.

One word of warning. Although the teens themselves did not mention this, it is my experience as a parent that trading or lending clothes invites trouble. Good clothing lost or damaged by a friend can result in hard feelings or even the end of a friendship. I suggest you include this rule in the guidelines you set for your teen.

Friends

A recent survey of teen priorities, taken among 14- and 15-year-olds, indicates that friends are the most important factor in teens' lives. This unscientific survey confirms what most people who work with teens already realize — that teens seek out their peers first. Unfortunately, most parents are either unaware of this fact, or refuse to believe it. This results in many arguments which otherwise would be preventable.

> **Teens seek out their peers first.**

Teen:	"Tania told me that you can get pregnant from a toilet seat."
Parent:	"Actually that's not true. Don't they teach you anything in Health classes?"
Teen:	"Well Tania says you can. She wouldn't lie to me."

It won't matter how many facts you quote at this point, if Tania said it, it must be true. In other words, when it comes to a difference of opinion between a parent and a peer, the peer wins every time.

Confirmation of peers' importance is seen dramatically when a parent tries to break up an "undesirable" friendship. The resulting conflict will approximate the Second World War, with less favorable results. The short answer is that it can't be done. Let's hear what Jamie has to say on the subject:

"The friends I have at my old school were the reason I changed schools. They are always in trouble. One just got kicked out of her home. Two of them are going to Juvenile Court. They are bad news, but they are still my friends. My parents forbid me to have anything to do with them. I do anyway."

A parent will almost always fail when trying to legislate friendships. Kids select their friends on the basis of having something in common, and cling to them until those common interests change. Fortunately these changes happen fairly often in the early teen years, especially with girls. However, until it does, parents can only grit their teeth and hope their child won't get hurt too badly. Parents need to understand that the teen is getting something important from the relationship and will resist all attempts to end it.

Many parents find the peer relationships frustrating or depressing, or both, and are sometimes jealous of them. After all, the parents have been the dominant force in their kids' lives to date, and it seems as if they are no longer needed. Teens feel parents don't understand their problems, and therefore won't ask them for help and advice. This is, at root, a communication problem, which will be dealt with in a later chapter. For now it is critical to understand the importance of friends to teens, and the hazards of interfering with those friendships.

So fine, teens think that peers are the most important element of their lives. What does this mean for parents? Mainly that you will now be able to use this understanding to (1) avoid conflict and (2) support your child when a friendship turns sour.

When parents announce on Thursday night that they have planned a ski trip for the weekend, they may be greeted by either silence or protest, rather than the anticipated delight. Parents may feel hurt and angry about the lack of enthusiasm, which leads in turn to a family argument. The teen's explanation for not wanting to go usually involves friends. Either plans have been made for a party or a movie, or the disappointment over not being with peers on the weekend outweighs the excitement of the ski trip. Parents must understand that these are normal feelings for teens and negotiate, rather than get angry. A compromise might be, "How about coming with us this weekend, and next week you can choose what you want to do?" Or, if the teen has already made plans it might be wise to say, "Okay, let's see if you can stay over at a friend's, but next trip we'll do the family thing." The key is to **stay cool** and not take the refusal personally. The teen is not rejecting the parents so much as fulfilling a powerful need to be with their own age group.

Another ticklish situation occurs when your teen begins to associate with someone you don't trust. Many parents believe, or want to believe, that the apparently untrustworthy friend has some sort of hold over their naive child. This is rarely the case. Realize that, for the friendship to last, your child must be getting something out of it. Thus, an obvious attempt to break up this closeness will be fiercely resisted. Patience is the key. If the friend really is a bad influence, and your child has no serious stability problems, then the companion's true nature will eventually be revealed, and the ties will wither. As Ryan says:

"Don't resist against anything too hard because it just makes them want it more."

Changing friends is common in the early teen years, especially among girls. Often the maturation process moves faster in one teen than in another, which leads to changing interests. If one young woman becomes interested in boys, while her friend remains disinterested, conflicts result. Suddenly the old friend seems boring, and a gradual shift to others with the same interests occurs. This leaves the teen left behind hurt and confused. She wonders what is the matter with her. At this stage, parents become important. By helping their daughter understand she has done nothing wrong, and conveying this to her, parents can ease the pain.

Why does this situation happen more frequently with girls? Hormonal changes of puberty happen quickly in females. The changes occur much more gradually in males, allowing the interests of most members of the male group to transform at nearly the same time.

Whatever the reason, awareness of this unevenness in maturing, and your ability to communicate it to the hurt teen, can help ensure a close relationship between parent and child.

Independence

This is another area to be aware of in understanding your teen. What they mean by "freedom" and "independence" is the right to make some decisions on their own, and the right not to be closely questioned about everything they do. Mixed in with these basics are wishes for extended curfews, rights to attend parties and dances, and the desire for privacy.

Mother:	"Where are you going?"
Beth:	"To the mall."
Mother:	"What for?"
Beth:	"Oh, just to look around."
Mother:	"Who are you going with?"

Beth:	"Just some friends."
Mother:	"What friends?"
Beth:	"I don't know yet — Erica and some others."
Mother:	"I don't see why you're always running off to that mall if you're not going to buy anything. You should be doing homework anyway."
Beth:	"C'mon Mom, it's Saturday. Why do you have to ask all these questions anyway?"

... and the argument begins.

While mom's questions in this example are logical, Beth feels that they infringe on her freedom and interfere with her growing need for independence. Mom definitely has a right to know where Beth is going, with whom, and when she will be home, but other questions and concerns are best left unasked. Even the key questions should be asked in as casual a manner as possible — as if mom is interested but the matter is not all that important. If it starts to seem like the third degree, an argument is sure to result.

The same is true of other activities like parties, dances and movies. Teens want the minimum of apparent controls and the maximum number of their own decisions. Obviously a balance has to be struck. Teens are rarely capable of handling as much freedom as they ask for, and interestingly enough, they don't want as much as they ask for. Like discipline, they want some controls and they want to know that their parents care about them. Simply put, they want the controls to be much more subtle than in their pre-teen days.

> **Key questions should be asked in as casual a manner as possible.**

Jamie, a 15-year-old honor student, states these desires when she writes that she wants to:

"...be where I want, when I want without them bugging me and getting mad. I want to pick my own friends and

*hang out with who I want to, not who my parents want
me to. And I want the chance to prove I am responsible
and/or trustworthy."*

Clearly, a responsible parent would not be able to grant this much freedom. It is possible, though, to come close enough to make everyone happy through negotiation and compromise.

Part of the independence teens want is the right to be by themselves occasionally, to have some privacy. Despite being highly social beings, or maybe because of it, teens need time alone. For some reason this bothers parents. Many resent it when the teen closes the bedroom door. What is she doing in there? There may also be some disappointment that the child does not want to be with the family. Whatever the reason, resentment like this is a breeding ground for major battles. Shannon writes:

*"Me and my Dad got in a minor argument and I
slammed a cupboard because I was angry. Then he said
if I slammed anything ever again he'd take my door off
forever. So I was really mad by this time because he'd
overreacted so I slammed my door out of spite. Then he
took off my door for a week, and since I had no privacy
I slept in a sleeping bag on my bathroom floor."*

This anecdote not only shows the lengths teens will go to for some privacy, it shows how illogical parents can be under the influence of emotion. Every teen needs privacy sometimes. If the need is constant, with the teen hardly ever emerging from the bedroom, there is likely a problem. There will be other signs to accompany this self-imposed isolation, like a total lack of communication with parents or friends. In most cases, recognizing that the need for privacy is normal for a teen will avoid upset and potential conflict.

Bedrooms

To a teen, his or her own bedroom is the most important room in the house. Their bedrooms provide privacy and are also a space they can

stamp with the identity they are trying so hard to establish. Identity is realized through "decor," which usually means posters and pictures cut or torn from magazines. It is also a place where they can play music without censorship (unless it gets too loud).

Recognizing the importance of this space is vital to a good relationship between parent and teenager. Allow considerable latitude in decorating and furniture arrangement, so that the room is a comfortable place for them. Standards of good taste may require negotiation. After all, it is your house. But discussion and coming to a consensus works better than telling the teen what can or cannot be tacked onto the bedroom wall. As far as possible, let the bedroom be the teen's own space.

> **A teen's own bedroom is the most important room in the house.**

A teen's sleeping area is not known as the "disaster area" or "garbage dump" without cause. It is the rare teenager who keeps a bedroom clean without prompting. Tidiness and organizational ability do not seem to be natural characteristics of most adolescents. One exception to this general rule I know of is a teen who had her clothes closet organized by color, with each hanger spaced an identical distance apart. This teen may have been one to worry about. The perfectionist has far more difficulty learning to accept disorder than the messy teen has learning to organize.

For the parent, the answer again is patience, persistence, and a touch of humor. Understand that messiness is typical, but maintain your personal standards. Some sort of compromise can be worked out whereby a certain amount of messiness is tolerated, but within limits. For example, as long as the bedroom is not unhygienic, with food and dirty dishes lying around, then the mess can be tolerated until the weekend, when a general clean-up can take place. And, normally, there will be resistance to this chore. This is where persistence and humor are vital. Don't get mad. Keep reminding until the job is done. You cannot assume that it will be done. Monitor the situation calmly, until you are satisfied.

> **Kids still want to know the family is there for them when they need it.**

Family

Surprised? Almost equal in importance to freedom and independence for a teen is the family. Jamie, who wrote so strongly about the desire for freedom from parental controls, stated in her next paragraph that she would like to see more of her dad. Teens need their parents' love and support, more than ever before — but they don't want it to be too obvious. Despite all the frustrations and arguments between parents and their teenaged children, kids still want to know the family is there for them when they need it — and they will need it a lot in the years ahead. At the same time, they would like parental control to be less obvious — a difficult adjustment for some parents because it means letting go a little. You will have to get used to letting go, because gradually you will have to, more and more.

Don't stop planning family outings because your teen always protests when informed of them. The protests are more a result of not having any input into the decision, or of having already made plans with friends, than a rejection of the idea. Fred writes:

"I always try to plan something and my parents plan something else, and they expect me to cancel my plans for theirs."

The family is still important to the average teen, it just doesn't rank as number one. Adrienne, a recent immigrant, records her thoughts:

"To me my family is important and my friends are important. My friends are really important to me because sometimes they understand my problems and it's because they are my age."

Denise echoes these feelings when she writes:

"The most important things to me are my sports and my friends. My family is important and all, it's just they're not my age and don't like doing the same things."

Understanding is part of the "Hear Me" in the "Hear Me, Hug Me, Trust Me" approach because it involves considerable listening, like why a teen wants to wear certain clothes, why they'd rather be with their friends, and why they caved in to peer pressure.

UNDERSTANDING YOUR TEEN

- Remember how you felt when you were a teen.
- Talk to other parents of teens.
- Really listen to what they are saying.
- Remember that they need some privacy and independence.
- Respect their choices — of friends, music, and even clothing.

2

The Sounds
of Silence

**⟨⟨ It's easy to talk to parents if they listen
instead of yelling and getting mad. ⟩⟩**
– Crystal

2. Improve COMMUNICATION

Right at the top of the teen's list is the ability to communicate with their parents. It is probably *the* most important element in establishing and maintaining good relations with your child. Nausheen describes ideal parents as "parents who can listen, and parents who can talk to their children about anything."

At the top of Alison's list of ideal traits is "to be able to talk to your parent and feel comfortable about it" and "to be able to make decisions together, not just the parent."

What is it about communication that makes it the basis for the parent/teen relationship? It has to do with the insecurity of teenagers. Teens may no longer be the dependent little tadpoles they once were, but despite the "I can handle anything" act they put on and their attempts to gain independence, they find life confusing. The plain truth is that teens rely on their parents when times become difficult.

The majority of the situations that confront teens involve social predicaments, such as fights with friends or the break-up of a relationship. A predicament might involve losing a big game or competition or failing a test at school. When these things happen, teens need someone to confide in, someone to look to for support. Even though at this age they turn to their friends first, their peers don't usually have the insight and experience to solve the problem. Parents often do. If the teen feels comfortable in discussing their problems with parents, then they feel a sense of security, and this brings them closer. Even if they don't talk about anything important, the knowledge that they can if they have to gives them a warm feeling. Mike very wisely writes:

> *"A teen will try to converse with you on a topic that has almost nothing to do with his life or anyone else's, but listen to him. This will help open up the passageways for future communication."*

Communication is a major part of a teenager's self-esteem. If parents are willing to take the time to listen, to comfort them, and maybe to give some useful advice, the teen feels worthwhile. This sense of worth is part of the teen's concept of how good a person he or she is, that is, of the *self-image.* If the teen can easily talk about relatively trivial things, such as daily events, TV programs and sports, then when the time comes they will be able to discuss major events such as fights with friends, school problems and even sexual matters.

Unfortunately, the ability to communicate with teens does not come easily to most people, and therefore the skills must be learned. But these skills can be learned in time to make a difference in your relationship with your teen.

Before discussing how to communicate with teens, we will look first at the process of communication, and at the difference between discussions with a teen and with an adult.

WHAT KIND OF COMMUNICATION WORKS?

"My parents let me talk first, and they don't jump in when I'm trying to say something." – Sarah

Communication is defined in the Oxford Dictionary partly as imparting, giving or sharing information. This definition is only the start of true communication. Oxford says nothing about timing; that is, when this sharing process should occur.

In old cowboy films, messages were sent and received on the telegraph in Morse code. Before an answer could be given whether the stagecoach had arrived with the gold, the telegrapher had to wait for the entire message to be completed, because the line was tied up with the incoming question. This is called half-duplex communication because it can only go one way at a time. Modern electronic systems, like the telephone, allow for duplex communication, which means that information can go both ways simultaneously. This means the ability to interrupt the incoming material, possibly for clarification, or even for both parties to talk at the same time (not generally a useful process).

Discussions with teens (or anyone else for that matter) can be either half-duplex, with one person waiting until the other is completely finished talking before beginning; or duplex, with interruptions and/or both parties talking at the same time.

In the case of teens, the half-duplex system works best. In fact, much of the time teens are only looking for half-duplex communication — they want to do the talking, and need someone to listen. To them, if you become a good listener, then you're a great communicator.

> **To teens, if you become a good listener, then you're a great communicator.**

THE PARENT HAS TO STAY CALM

Even when a parent is on half-duplex, communicating with teens remains difficult because of the age gap. It doesn't take a rocket scientist to figure that out, but it does help to keep this in mind.

It is the emotional, insecure nature of most teenagers that results in barriers to effective communication. They are highly defensive, quick to anger when disagreed with and already know everything. This makes discussing anything like walking on eggs — you do it very carefully or the situation is quickly scrambled. And remember the concept of "Who's in control." It is vital in any discussion that one side remains calm. You can bet it won't be the teenager.

LISTENING

"My parents never listen to what I say. My little sister might start crying for no reason, say it was me and then I get into trouble. I try to explain and say I didn't do it. But they let her get away with murder. It drives me nuts." – Mira

Setting the Scene

Most teens surveyed said something similar to Mira — namely, that their parents don't listen to them. The starting point of communicating with teens, then, appears to be being a good listener. Since listening is difficult when distractions are present, the starting point of listening is setting the scene so that the teen has the opportunity to talk. Sometimes a good discussion can happen spontaneously, but most often you have to structure your family life to allow for conversation.

THE SUPPER TABLE

The best of all places for conversation is at the supper table. Once the meal is on the table and everyone has sat down, you can relax. Suddenly the worries of the day disappear (at least temporarily), and everyone can be themselves. At this point the family can talk about the day's happenings and exchange information. This won't necessarily happen by itself. Someone, usually a parent, has to ask a question or make an observation to get things going, but once started a momentum will develop to keep things moving. The key is that the family is together in a relatively relaxed setting.

Unfortunately this does not happen as often as it once did. With both parents working in most households, many families have abandoned this tradition. Kids often make their own meals, and parents have theirs when they get home. If at all possible, avoid this trap. The evening meal is by far the best place to develop and maintain family communication.

HOUSEHOLD CHORES

Another good communication opportunity is available through household chores. While this idea may, at first, seem a bit strange — given most teenagers' aversion to work — let's take a look at it. The various tasks concerning supper are a good example. Besides cooking, the table has to be set and the dishwasher may have to be emptied. After supper, the table has to be cleared, the dishwasher loaded, and the pots and pans washed and put away. These tasks can be done in teams, the composition of which depend on family size, but a team should have one adult and at least one child. Teamwork provides conversational opportunities, while getting jobs done faster. Other household duties, such as raking the lawn, folding the laundry, or washing the car, present similar opportunities. If given a chance to talk, most teens will take it. In my experience, children enjoy talking to their parents, unless parents indicate through actions or words they aren't interested — usually by not listening — or block communication.

TAXI SERVICE

An excellent time for having a meaningful conversation comes when driving teens to such places as lessons, the mall or to school. When there is just a parent and a teen in the vehicle, uninterrupted discussion is possible. You have a captive audience. So, rather than considering taxi service a chore, see it as an opportunity to talk.

Other opportunities present themselves unexpectedly — take them whenever you can. If you are passing the teen's bedroom and you see that she is staring into space, stop for a few minutes and try to get a conversation going. If your son is out in the yard idly shooting a few hoops, shoot a few with him, no matter how bad a basketball player you are. While playing, ask a few questions about his life. Show that the channels of communication are open.

Blocking the Flow

No matter how carefully a parent tries to set the scene for communication, conversation will stop immediately if not allowed to flow. There are several ways this happens.

INTERRUPTING

One of the fastest ways to end a discussion or conversation is to interrupt.

> *"I can't talk to my parents because they don't give me a chance to. I open my mouth to start to say something and I am interrupted by them giving me all this advice and their opinions. Basically a big lecture before I even have a chance to finish what I'm saying." – Rachel*

Even worse than interrupting to give advice is interrupting to make a point not related to the conversation.

> *"When I talk to my parents I always expect the worst. Even worse is when you do talk to them and they correct your grammar. I can't stand that." – Christy*

Another example is correcting one child's table manners while the other is telling a story, or complaining about the slang or swear words being used. Lisa makes this point when she states "Many parents forget the meaning of the conversation when a teen would accidentally let a swear slip out." If you feel you must, gently make these corrections, but **after** you have responded to the story. Don't interrupt if at all possible. The bottom line is that parents should concentrate on the *contents* of what is being said by the teen and not on *how* it is delivered.

> *Parents should concentrate on the contents of what is being said by the teen and not on* **how** *it is delivered.*

MAKING JUDGMENTS

Another way to kill a conversation is to quickly make a judgment or decision as to what happened or what should be done next.

Jake: "Mom, I failed my Math exam today."

Mom: "What!"

Jake: "Just listen."

Mom: "NO. You told me you studied. There's no way you did if you failed. Go to your room!"

There is now no way that the real explanation for the failure will come out, because Jake will be frustrated and angry. Instead of making a snap judgment, it would have been better to have calmly asked, "What went wrong?" Then mom should have listened to the whole answer before drawing a conclusion.

Linda, who feels she communicates well with her mother most of the time, agrees with Jake when she writes:

> *"It is sometimes hard to talk to her because she often jumps to conclusions. She often accuses me of things I didn't do or did to a minor degree and if she could just*

listen to my full side of the story instead of jumping to conclusions, I might be more willing to talk to her."

Another student, Tanya, who also feels she communicates well with her mother, phrases the situation more positively:

"I can talk to my Mom because she cares about what I think and sometimes she even asks for my opinion and then takes it into consideration before making a decision."

Finally, Nathan shows the effect when parents make judgments and do not listen, when he writes:

"It is hard to talk to my parents because they get their own idea of what they want or think is right and they won't listen to what I have to say. I can't talk to my parents and I don't."

Nathan's solution to this communication block is that his parents should "Listen to what I have to say and at least go along with some of what I have to say." Good advice.

SHOWING EMOTION

Some of the things teens tell their parents about are bound to arouse emotion. Failure at school, in Jake's case, got an immediate emotional response. Anger, disappointment, shock or even laughter in the wrong place can bring a quick death to a conversation—or lead to an argument.

Remaining unemotional can be very trying when your teen tells you something that shocks or scares you. For example, when you are told that your daughter's best friend was drunk at a weekend party, your mind is immediately filled with questions and fears. Was your daughter drinking too? Is there drinking at all the parties? What else goes on besides the drinking? While it is perfectly normal to be worried, *do not let it show*. If you ever want to find out what really goes on at these parties, you cannot blurt out your concerns — or your opinions. Instead, hide your feelings, stay calm, and *after* the teen has finished the story, ask one or two questions you feel you need to know.

There is nothing wrong with asking questions to learn more about your teen's world — in fact it's a good idea — but don't let your worry or disapproval stop the conversation. You can express your opinions if your child is involved in illegal, dangerous or unhealthy activities. In fact you should, to let them know where you stand morally. Do so as coolly as possible, so as not to end an open and frank discussion.

Kathryn, a bright but extremely independent young lady, proves that it isn't just anger and shock that can stop communication. She writes:

> *"My parents are hard to talk to about certain things because they laugh or tease me and they can't relate to what I say."*

Remember that, although teen problems may not seem serious in relation to adult ones, to them these concerns are life or death, and must be treated as such if you want them to be able to come to you with the really important issues. Vlad, who is from Russia, has the same concern. He states:

> *"My parents would probably laugh at my values, ideas. They wouldn't understand me. I always choose what to say so I won't get laughed at. And it's pretty hard."*

Isn't it interesting that teens from two different sides of the world have exactly the same problem. Erin finds that communication is improving with her mother because mom is not expressing anger. Erin writes:

> *"Well, I can talk to my mother more and more now. She understands and she doesn't explode. It makes life easier on me so I can feel more comfortable talking to her."*

From the number of teens who commented on the anger and explosion cause of communication blocks, it is apparent that there are lots of opportunities to get upset. Don't take them.

"It's hard when they think they're right and act like whatever you say is wrong. Most kids would love to talk to their parents about sex, drinking, drugs. But feel their parents would be disappointed. The parents should make it clear that they will love them whatever they do." – Kelly

What is Kelly's solution for better communication? Few adults could say it any better:

"Sit you down in a relaxed environment, don't look angry, don't be an adult. Talk one on one as equals."

NOT UNDERSTANDING

"I can't talk to my parents because they don't look at it from my point of view and they usually end up saying when I was your age I didn't do that or I was older when I started that. They haven't been kids for over 20 years and they don't realize things are different than when they were kids." – Carey

One of the ways to stop a conversation abruptly is to relate the topic under discussion to your childhood. Even if the point you are making is closely related to the situation, the chances are high that you will lose your audience. Today's teens don't want to hear about your teenage years because they consider them antiquated. While this is not always true, it is the case often enough. So try to avoid breaking into the teen's story to talk about your experience.

Listen to what Kristin has to say:

"I can't talk to my parents because they seem to be out of date. They don't seem to know what's happening. They always say 'Oh, when I was a teenager...' They don't know it's different now."

Shelly agrees completely:

"I can't talk to my Mom because she doesn't remember what it's like to be my age so she isn't able to understand why I feel like I do."

Nancy, a Grade 8 student, writes:

"It's hard to talk to them about personal things because I'm their 'little girl' and they don't want me to grow up. They get mad because they don't understand the new problems that teenagers face today. I can't talk to them at all whatsoever. I'm afraid to."

Rules for Listening to Teens

Listening is definitely the hard part of communication. To sum up the points made above, here are some guidelines for good listening.

1. Make it possible for the teen to talk to you by making family times available.
2. Don't interrupt.
3. Don't make snap judgments. Wait until you hear the entire story.
4. Try not to show emotion, including anger, disappointment or laughter.
5. No matter how relevant you think it is, don't relate the situation to your youth.
6. If told something in confidence, keep it to yourself.

Now wait a minute. Where did that last point come from? Confidentiality wasn't mentioned before. True, but listen to what Jackie says:

"When I talk to my dad he can't keep anything confidential. He will usually tell my sister what I said."

Information given in confidence by your teen can certainly be shared with your spouse, but keep it between the two of you. If a teen feels that everything said will be repeated, nothing will be said.

Here's a long final thought on listening from Linda, an obviously deep-thinking Grade 9 student:

"I wish they would hear the full side of the story from my point of view before opening fire on me with their side of the story. When they don't listen to me I could care less what they think of my problems because they don't understand them. They often compare my teenaged life to theirs and they have to stop doing that because a teenager in the 90's is different. They need to hear me out and trust my word and not accuse me. If they don't accuse me I'll tell them more anyway and they won't have to jump to conclusions. Parents just need to listen to what we have to say before making us hear what they have to say."

TALKING

As you may have gathered from the discussion above, listening is by far the more important part of communicating with teens. This doesn't mean that you must always maintain an icy calm silence. On the contrary, there are many times when it is vital that you do say something. Just as there are "rules" for listening, there are ways to talk to teens that will keep the channels of communication open. Other methods will only snap them shut. With a little practice, these channels can stay open most of the time.

Expanding the Conversation

Even with the family sitting down to a pleasant and relaxed dinner together, conversation will not flow automatically. In fact, unless you have an unusual teen, it will not flow at all. Don't let this discourage you — it's normal. Instead, practice the art of expanding conversation. The first rule is *"Never ask a question that can be answered in one word."* Such questions include:

- How was school? (Usual answer "Fine.")
- Do you have any homework? (Usual answer "No.")
- What's new? (Usual answer "Nothing.")
- What did you do at the mall? (Same as above.)

Ask more specific questions, such as:

- What did you do in Math today?
- How much homework do you have?
- Are there any good sales on at the mall?

I can hear you saying right now, "They can still give one-word answers to these questions," and you would be right. But it's a lot harder than with the first set. Also, the first question is only part of the technique. You have to follow up with more questions until the conversation gets going. To do this you have to keep up with what's happening in their lives. Let's look at some sample sessions.

You're all sitting at the dinner table and everyone has their food, when Mom attempts a conversation with Cari:

Mom:	"Did anything interesting happen in school today?"
Cari:	"Not really."
Mom:	"Well, how did you do in that Math assignment you were working on last night?"
Cari:	"Not too well. I only got 55."
Mom:	"Oh? Weren't you happy with that mark?"
Cari:	"No. The teacher marked really hard and took off marks for not showing my work, even though my answers were right."
Mom:	"Hasn't he done that before?"
Cari:	"No, this is the first time we've had this type of assignment."

There are several points to notice about this conversation. First, Mom didn't stop after the first short answer but pursued the subject. Next, Mom knew that Cari had been working on a Math assignment the night before. To know this she had to have been paying attention to what Cari was doing for homework. Third, Mom did not explode when she heard the low mark but instead asked an open-ended question. This ensures that in the future, when Cari gets a low mark, she won't be afraid to tell Mom about it. From this point Mom can get in a gently-worded commercial about making sure Cari shows all her work on the next Math assignment and presto — a conversation has taken place.

By way of explanation, kids do not give brief answers to questions just to annoy parents. Initially, until the questions force them to think about things, they really believe that nothing much happened. Let's look at another sample conversation between Dad, this time, and daughter Cari.

Dad:	"How's your friend Jeannie doing?" (Bad question, but he'll recover.)
Cari:	"Fine."
Dad:	"Didn't you have a fight with her yesterday?"

Cari: "Yes, but we straightened everything out."

Dad: "Oh, how did you do that?"

Cari: "Well, remember that she told Jodie who my boyfriend was? I just went over to her and asked her not to tell my secrets any more — and know what? She actually apologized and said it just slipped out, and she would be more careful next time. So we're friends again."

As in the previous conversation, Dad did not give up easily. He also had to be listening the night before when Cari mentioned the fight. With just three questions, Dad had the discussion proceeding smoothly.

Occasionally you will hit upon a topic that the teen does not want to discuss. If two or three questions all get short, uninformative answers, leave that topic alone. File it away in the back of your mind as a sensitive issue that may require discussion later in a more private setting, but don't pursue it. If you do you may be accused of nagging — or worse — an argument might start.

Talking Down

After listening, teenagers' next major concern in the communications area was with parents "talking down" to them. This means that the parents tend to *tell* them how to do things, rather than make suggestions. Talking down to teens in effect makes parents always right, an appearance that annoys teens. The fact is that parents are often right, but teens prefer a more collaborative approach. Once again, they would like some input into the solutions, rather than having parents make all the decisions for them. This fits right in with the teenagers' desire for more independence, and to be considered more adult.

> *"I can talk to my parents because they talk to me as if I'm an equal (usually). They listen to me and they give*

advice as best as they can. They don't usually tell me what to do about something." – Melanie

When Vlad was asked how he thought his parents should communicate with him he wrote:

"I suggest they would talk to me as equal, not as a kid. Very often they send me to sleep early or command me to do something. I think it would be way easier or more effective to just talk reasonable or as equal. I'm not a kid anymore, I'm a teenager. My parents still don't understand that."

Susan agrees completely, and has obviously put some thought into the matter:

"I can talk to my parents because we talk on a friend-like basis rather than a parent to child, one which makes it easier for both of us to communicate. I am able to tell my parents things as though they were my friends and even if they don't understand things I tell them, we discuss them until they can at least make sense out of what I am saying. I think it's a real privilege to be able to talk openly with your parents, because it helps them understand you and what you're going through better and for you to understand your parents and why they do what they do."

Now, when teens say that they should be able to talk to their parents as friends, this does not mean that they want parents to be friends. They still want them in the parent role, as we'll see in the next chapter. What they mean is they want to be able to talk to parents in the same way that they can talk to friends. They don't want the parent to be telling them what to do, but instead to listen carefully, then suggest ways of dealing with situations. Instead of saying, "When I was a teenager we did things this way and that's how it should be," the parent might say, "Why don't you try doing it this way?"

Another habit many parents have which immediately labels them as the superior member of the conversation, is to deny their teens' ideas or feelings. This occurs when the teen makes a remark or comment and the parent says "You don't mean that," or "That's not true." Here's a sample conversation from Gillian's home:

> Gillian: "I think my teacher hates me."
>
> Mom: "No he doesn't. Nobody's teacher hates them!"

This effectively ended the conversation by denying the teen's point of view. The teen usually becomes defensive and refuses to talk any more. Again, it is far more productive to adopt a more open approach such as:

> Gillian: "I think my teacher hates me."
>
> Mom: "What did he do to give you that impression?"

This will keep the conversation flowing, and may even end with the teen seeing things from mom's point of view.

If you can converse with your teen without taking the expert's position, and instead approach the discussion as just another participant, the youngsters tend to listen much better, and even appreciate your viewpoint.

Nagging

> *"Parents nag teens always, it's in their blood to nag. Nagging to do chores, nagging to do homework, take a shower, walk the dog, it's always something like that." – Craig*

In Craig's opinion, nagging is a genetic quality that expresses itself as soon as a person becomes a parent. It is not a major concern of teens — they seem to agree with Craig that nagging is part of being a parent. In fact it came up in the surveys only a few times. Nagging does, however, lead to arguments and rebellious behavior if overdone, and should be avoided wherever possible. Sabrina shows how she resents it when she writes (in run-on sentence form):

> *"My parents are real easy to talk to — depending on the time of day, mornings all you get is grunts or nagging (have you done all your homework, have you got everything, where are you going after school, etc.)."*

The definition of "nagging" varies with the teen's need for independence. Some resent just one reminder that they have not done some chore or commitment. Others do not get upset until the third or fourth reminder. It's a parent's responsibility to check on whether a chore has been done or to remind their kids that something has not yet been finished. When one reminder is not enough — the job still hasn't been done — the parent has to become more creative. Humor is far more effective in these situations than an angry reminder. An effective technique, one that Craig recommends, is to leave notes in prominent places, again using humor whenever possible. (There will be more on how to get jobs done without causing an argument, both in Chapter 7 and Chapter 10.

Yelling

Frustration is, at times, expressed by yelling, as if this will help make the point clearer. No matter who starts yelling — the parent or teen — communication ends quickly. Few parental communication methods are more resented than the raising of voices. When questioned about how she suggests parents communicate with her, Erin says, "Talk with me when they have a problem, not yell at me." Courtney's suggestion for better communication is "Through talking calmly not yelling and getting upset." Sarah likes the way her parents talk with her:

> *"I think they communicate very well and are always calm. They don't yell and if we are in a bad mood they*

understand and calm us down and talk to us in a normal tone of voice, they never raise it."

"It's much easier for teens to listen to what their parents say if they talk and don't yell. Yelling only makes the child feel worse off than before." – Crystal

Showing negative emotion while listening stops communication cold. Yelling when trying to make a point has exactly the same effect. Like the tourist in a foreign country who is not understood, the frustrated parent tries to be understood by saying it louder.

When voices are raised, emotions are too, and whenever a situation becomes emotional, nothing gets resolved. The "Who's the parent?" question crops up again. Even if the teen starts yelling, the parent must remain calm if the situation is to be straightened out. Sam sums this up by saying:

"I think the ideal parents are those who take things in stride. They shouldn't yell at their kid at everything they do wrong. The parents should be in control of their kids too."

In other words, the parent is the adult and has to stay in control.

HOW TO HANDLE AN ARGUMENT

Obviously the best way to handle an argument is not to let one begin. By maintaining an understanding of the explosive nature of teens, by using humor to diffuse difficult situations, and by staying calm when your teen erupts, arguments won't happen often. Being human, however, we don't always do things perfectly and disagreements will occur even in the best of households.

Fatigue is the main culprit. After a difficult day at the office, it's hard to stay cool when you open the door to the kitchen garbage container and it overflows on your feet — again. The tendency is to bellow at the guilty party, who then reacts defensively, and the battle is on.

The scary thing about arguments is that they don't stay on the disputed topic — in this case the garbage. Instead they quickly go downhill into personal attacks. The parent makes statements like "you *never* take the garbage out," or "you're *always* lazy."

The teen responds with "you *never* give me any credit for what I do," or "you're *always* in a bad mood." Strong emotions are aroused. Once voices are raised, the intention of both sides is to upset the other party — possibly to try to make a point through shock tactics. It doesn't work. Once angry, neither side listens. The result is not only an immediate ugly scene, but a stressful time for days afterwards.

Even if your angry side shows and you fail to remain calm, get control of the discussion as soon as possible. If you have already shouted, and been shouted back at, suck back and reload. Take a deep breath, pause for a few seconds, then start fresh. Let's look at the example of taking out the garbage.

Dad:	[in a loud, angry voice] "Kevin, get down here this minute!"
Kevin:	[in a snotty tone of voice] "What's the matter now!"
Dad:	[still loudly] "You didn't take the garbage out again. It's falling all over the floor."
Kevin:	"Chill out. I'll take it out later."
Dad:	"You'll take it out NOW! Why are you always so lazy?"
Kevin:	"Why are you always on my case? I do stuff around here all the time and you never say thanks or anything. I miss just once and you start screaming."
Dad:	"I'll scream if I want to. Unless you start being more responsible, you can find someplace else to live!"
Kevin:	"Fine. I'd rather live in the streets than with you!" (He storms into his room and slams the door.)

Does this sound familiar? The yelling, the generalizations (you always..., you never...) and finally the statements that aren't meant. There are three places where this argument could have been controlled:

1. Right at the start. If Dad had not yelled or had not been obviously angry, he likely wouldn't have gotten a snarky answer. Emotion is usually responded to emotionally. If he had calmly called Kevin to the kitchen and asked him to please remember to take the garbage out, he might only have received a sigh or a mumbling. That, though, would be the perfect Dad — on certain days, most of the rest of us would have yelled too.

2. After yelling that Kevin should take out the garbage immediately. The point has now been made. It's time to take a deep breath, pause, and get control of the situation. At this instant, having read the Introduction, and understanding that teens are insecure, defensive organisms, Dad can expect the emotional response and be ready for it. The response is not really a personal attack on Dad, but a defense against what Kevin sees as an attack on him. Really, it's not an attack by anyone, Dad just wants the garbage taken out regularly. As soon as the parent recognizes that an argument is starting, it's time to settle things down.

3. After Kevin complains about the "screaming." Some generalizations have taken place, but no real harm has been done. There is still time for Dad to keep the situation from degenerating into the hurtful stage. Again the technique involves realizing what is happening, taking a deep breath — or even just taking a short pause — then asking Kevin to please just take the garbage out, and try to remember it's his job.

> **Realize when the situation is becoming overly emotional, and get control as soon as possible.**

Understanding the teenager's insecurity is the key. They don't like yelling and they usually react defensively to the implication that they have failed. Parents have to understand that when teens respond in an angry or sullen tone of voice, in most instances they are not trying to upset you. Nor have the parents failed to teach responsibility or manners. This is a normal response, so parents should treat it as such and not take the tone of voice personally. Instead, realize when the situation is becoming overly emotional, and get control as soon as possible. With this knowledge, let's replay the scene, and take control at point 2.

Dad: [in a loud, angry voice] "Kevin get down here this minute!"

Kevin: [in a snotty tone of voice] "What's the matter now?"

Dad: [still loudly] "You didn't take the garbage out again. It's falling all over the floor."

Kevin: "Chill out. I'll take it out later."

Dad: [deep breath and pause] "Could you come down and do it right away so you don't forget?"

Kevin: [still not too happy, but...] "All right. I'm coming."

If the situation gets to point 3 before he realizes that a big argument is coming, Dad would probably be wise to add an apology. It might sound like this:

Dad: [in a loud, angry voice] "Kevin get down here this minute!"

Kevin: [in a snotty tone of voice] "What's the matter now!"

Dad: [still loudly] "You didn't take the garbage out again. It's falling all over the floor."

Kevin: "Chill out. I'll take it out later."

Dad: "You'll take it out NOW! Why are you always so lazy?"

Kevin: "Why are you always on my case! I do stuff around here all the time and you never say thanks or anything. I miss just once and you start screaming."

Dad: [deep breath — slightly longer pause to regain control] "Hold on. Sorry about the lazy bit, but it is frustrating to find this mess after a long day. Could you come down and take it out right away — before you forget?"

Kevin: "Yeah, well you don't have to shout all the time. I'm coming."

The longer the argument goes on, the harder it is to gain control. This control is well worth getting, though, to avoid saying things that aren't meant and the three days of not speaking that usually results from ill-chosen words.

LECTURING

This section could well be subtitled "How to get a teen to tune out quickly." There is no faster way to ensure being tuned out than by launching into a lengthy lecture on some righteous theme. It's hard to say why many adults feel that a point is made more effectively by repeating it several times in different words. Whatever the reason, it's a common tendency when the inevitable happens and your teen makes a mistake. (This might be coming home late from school or a party, getting a poor mark on a test or failing to do a chore.) When surveyed, students reported lectures ranging from a few minutes to an hour and a half. As Diana says:

"Why do they think they have to say the same thing ten different ways? I got it the first time."

The tendency to lecture sometimes comes from the fact that when they know they did something wrong, teens don't usually say much. The lack of response is often interpreted as either not understanding that they did something wrong, or even as dumb defiance. The parent goes over and over the point until it is felt that the teen understands, or until the parent becomes exhausted — whichever comes first.

Another possible explanation for lecturing is that, when worried, parents need to blow off some steam, and take the opportunity to do it on the offender. Whatever the reason, it doesn't help. The most effective sequence of events when something goes wrong is to listen to the teen's explanation, briefly state why you are upset, then hand out the consequences, if required. End it there and you avoid the risk of the teen tuning out, or worse, looking bored or saying something rude, which makes the parent even more angry.

WHEN THEY'RE UPSET

Back in the section on expanding the conversation, I mentioned that sometimes teens don't want to talk. If this is the case, it's usually best not to push the point — especially if there are other family members around. Instead, wait until you can talk to the teen undisturbed, such as when he or she is doing homework or, even better, when the teen is in bed, just about to turn out the light. Then you can sit on the edge of the bed and refer to when you first noticed the problem. You may have to dig a little, but almost always the teen really does want to talk, they just don't know how to get started. Let's look at a sample conversation to clarify this point.

> Mom: [coming into bedroom and sitting down]
>   "Are you all right, Jen, I noticed you
>   seemed a bit down at supper?
>
> Jen: "I'm fine."
>
> Mom: "Are you sure? You didn't say a thing all
>   through the meal."

Jen: "Well, I did have a problem in Science today."

Mom: "With the subject or with the teacher?"

Jen: "With the teacher. You know that project I spent four hours working on? He said it was all wrong, but he didn't say what was wrong with it."

Mom: "Did you talk to him after class or after school?"

Jen: "No. He was too busy, and I was too upset to talk to him anyway."

Mom: "Will you be able to talk to him tomorrow, or do you want one of us to call him?"

Jen: "I'll try to talk to him tomorrow, and if that doesn't work you can try."

There are several things to note about this conversation. Mom noticed the lack of communication during the meal, waited for a time when there were no distractions, then probed until she got to the source of her daughter's silence. When she found out the nature of the difficulty, she didn't jump to any conclusions about who was right or wrong, but looked for ways to solve the problem. Parents need to be observant and gently persistent to get teens to talk, and this persistence usually pays off in meaningful discussion.

There should be no doubt now about the importance of the "Hear Me" part of this book's title. Parental listening is a key ingredient of strong parent-teen relationships, of understanding teens, of helping to solve their problems and, as we'll see in the next chapter, of sorting out disciplinary situations.

LINES TEENS HATE TO HEAR

Here, in no particular order, are some of the lines that teens say they absolutely hate to hear:

- because I said so.
- because it's our house.
- you don't have a say in this.
- this is none of your business.
- you're too young to understand.
- when I was your age.
- I don't need a reason.
- kids today ...
- you ungrateful little ...
- don't talk back.
- I don't have time to talk about this right now.
- go ask your mother/father.
- you'll understand in a few years.

All of these are conversation stoppers or, worse, lead to tempers flaring. Avoid them if at all possible.

3

Ground Rules

**《《 The perfect parents are ones
who are strict but fair. 》》**
– Steve

3. Provide appropriate DISCIPLINE

Chapter 2 shows that communication is the foundation of a solid relationship with your teen. However, disciplinary situations, and how you handle them, can be the earthquakes which threaten even a solid foundation. While English teachers everywhere are probably cringing at this metaphor, the point is that all your efforts to develop a relationship can be weakened, even destroyed, by the rules that you set; inconsistent enforcement of them; or by a poor choice of consequences.

The weakening of the relationship with your teen is a result of anger and resentment building up inside them. This anger frequently erupts when decisions are made that they consider unfair. Teens evaluate every decision against *their* standards of fairness, and if the decisions come up short, they either explode or smolder with resentment.

HOW MUCH DISCIPLINE?

Steve's comment was echoed by most of the teens as they designed their "ideal parents." The attributes of "strict but fair" came up most often. It's apparent that teens really *want* a set of rules, and incredibly, they actually want consequences when they break these rules. Deep inside, they know that rules and subsequent consequences mean their parents care about them. They get a feeling of security by knowing where their limits are. What's that — you don't believe teens would say things like this? Check the quotes following for some proof of these statements.

> *"My parents aren't strict enough. (I can't believe I said that.) I can tell now that I will grow up warped and confused." – Rob*

> *"My parents are too easy on us ... they rarely do any severe punishment. As a result my siblings are greedy."*
> *– Hasyn*

> *"My parents' methods of discipline is not strict enough. My mom lets me get away with too much and doesn't do anything about it. A good punishment for me would be to take away my TV privileges." – Jeff*

> *"My parents are strict in a sense and set out their rules early. Now they are easing up. I think it's good because some parents let kids get away with a lot and if the kid gets away with it once they'll either try it again or do something worse because they know they won't get into much trouble." – Kathryn*

Now, here is where the other shoe drops — fairness. While Chapter 4 examines fairness more closely, fairness is:

- allowing the teen some input into setting rules and consequences
- allowing some flexibility in the enforcement of rules

- listening to the teen's side before deciding on a consequence

This doesn't seem too much to ask but it's amazing how many parents have trouble with the fairness part of the system.

RULES

Setting the Rules

> *"I think they can be pretty fair about thinking over my reasons for doing things and then talking with me about it until we've come to an agreement, like my curfew. What I really hate is when I ask my parents if I can do something and they say 'no' without giving me a reason. I ask why and they say 'just because.' That really makes me mad." – Kristina*

As children get older and move into their teen years, they want and need more freedom to stay out later, to go places without parental supervision, and to spend money. This freedom, however, is still a bit frightening for most teens and as we have seen from the above comments, while they want more freedom, they also want limits. Limits take the form of rules. The challenge is to set rules that everyone in the family is comfortable with.

> **The challenge is to set rules that everyone in the family is comfortable with.**

To set these rules, hold a short family meeting where both sides listen. Keep the rule list short — too many rules are confusing — and cover the areas where conflicts are most frequent, such as curfews, chores, the telephone and homework. The resulting brief list will be a compromise between two viewpoints.

> *"My parents are too protective. The rules they use seem pointless, like I'm not allowed to watch soaps when I get home from school, for no other reason than they say they are dumb." – Linda*

"I think that some rules are fair, but sometimes my parents don't even listen to my side of the story. They seem to hardly let me be free. My parents rarely let me use the phone, and for only short times. They don't seem to understand this and don't treat me as a young adult." – *Jennifer*

Compromising means first listening to what the teen wants, then setting a rule somewhere in between the teen's idea of fairness and yours. This process can be uncomfortable for parents because it means giving more freedom or privileges than you want to and taking some risks. For example, if parents suggest a curfew of 11:30 on a weekend, and the teen asks for 12:30, the obvious compromise time would be 12:00. While half an hour is not much time, caring parents have an extra 30 minutes to worry about the safe return of their teen. This is initially a difficult adjustment.

> *Compromising means first listening to what the teen wants, then setting a rule somewhere in between the teen's idea of fairness and yours.*

How Rules Usually Get Set

Unfortunately, most rules are set as a result of disagreements. Consider the following:

Dad: "Get off the phone, you've been talking for over an hour."

Linda: "But Dad, this is important."

Dad: "I said get off — you haven't done your homework yet."

Linda: "I don't have much, and Krista has a problem."

Dad: "That's it. From now on you're restricted to 20 minutes a night."

HOW TO SET RULES

As your teen becomes more socially active, there will be more and more requests for privileges. Once you notice this, hold a short meeting with your partner and your teen (preferably right after supper when everyone is in a good mood). Then follow these steps:

1. *Decide what areas to cover.* Usually you should include curfews, both week nights and weekends (hint: these should be different), homework time, telephone, bedroom and other chores, and dating (if this is becoming a factor). Keep the number of areas as low as possible; just touch on the major areas.

2. *For each area, ask what the teen wants first.* If the request is unreasonable, suggest an alternative. **Come to an agreement before moving on to the next item.**

3. *Make sure there is a clear reason for each rule.* If teens understand why a rule exists, they will have much less trouble following it.

4. *Once in place, don't change the rules.* Unless the teen clearly shows that the rule cannot be followed, usually by repeatedly breaking one, do not change anything for at least a year.

Writing up a list of the rules and posting it is a little too formal. The teen often sees it as an insult. If you keep the rules simple, everyone can remember them, and you can gently remind your teen at the appropriate times.

Ensuring Fairness

> *"Dad says I can't do certain things. It's unfair because he never says why. He beats around the bush and never gives me a straight answer. That's unfair to me."*
> *– Kristin*

Many parents are not quite sure how much rope to give their teen. What is a fair time to be in on a weekend? Should the teen be allowed out on week nights? How much phone time is enough?

You have an advantage over Moses in this area — the rules are not written in stone. There can't be any universal rule because times change and teens are individuals. For example, if your teenager is struggling at school, it only makes sense to have regular study times on week nights. An A+ whiz kid may not need such a rule. Some 12-year-olds are still playing with their toys, while others are actively interested in the opposite sex. This difference between teens means that variation in rules is required to reflect this individuality.

To set rules as fairly as possible, the networking method suggested in Chapter 1 can be helpful. At school or church functions, ask other parents what their rules are. Call the parents of your teen's friends and check out their standards. If you are really desperate, ask a relative with kids your age. Consider what Kristina has to say about her rules:

> *"My parents have trouble with curfews. Most of my friends except Jen can be out till about 11:30 p.m. I have to be in by 9:00 p.m."*

If your teen hits you with a statement like this, how do you know whether it's true or an exaggeration? Check it out. If you are way out of line, maybe you should bend a little. Checking with others would help you deal with a statement like Sara's:

> *"They don't let me do anything. Won't let me have a boy-friend until I'm 15 or in Grade 10, whichever comes first."*

Sara is obviously upset by this rule, but whether it's fair or not is a tough question. (Hint: How do you enforce it?)

This is not to say that your family has to have rules like everyone else's. It is still your family. But you will probably have more arguments, sulking and the kind of resentment shown by Sara, if your rules are much stricter than the majority of parents' in your child's age group.

Renegotiating

"If I were my parents I wouldn't be so overprotective. The curfews they set for me suck. It is always too early and I am usually the first to come home out of all my friends." – Kris

Setting rules for teens is not like a bar mitzvah, happening automatically when the child turns 13. Instead, it is a gradual process that develops as the need arises. For example, limits on telephone use usually are set when parents think their child is spending too much time talking on the phone, or when callers start having difficulty getting through. Once a number of rules are in place, they need to be renegotiated on a regular basis, since as teens

> **Rules need to be renegotiated as teens get older.**

get older, they are ready for more freedom and responsibility. Their social lives also become more complex as dating and mixed parties begin, and as they obtain the (dreaded) driver's license.

Unless they feel comfortable talking to their parents, most teens are reluctant to ask for changes. It's a big relief when the subject is brought up by the parents. Consider Michael's statement about his rules as an example:

"Some are fair, but most aren't. Things like my bedtime. I'm 16 years old and I still have to go to bed at 9:30 p.m. I've been going to bed at this time since I was 12 years old."

If Mike's parents saw this they would probably say, "Why didn't you say something?" He obviously has not felt comfortable discussing the subject, so he just burns internally. In most homes nothing changes until a new situation arises, like a school dance, or there is a major blowup because a rule is broken. In the latter case, the change may be deeply resented because the rule has been set in anger (and is therefore stricter than it might have been) and the teen had no say in the matter.

Therefore, it is a good idea to sit down with your teen on a yearly basis and revisit the major rules. The start of each school year provides an excellent reason for such a meeting, because it is a time of renewal, a fresh start. As a group you may decide that no changes are necessary. On the other hand, some rules may need updating. Whatever the case, renegotiating works best if you first let the teen state what changes he or she desires. You will often be surprised at how reasonable the demands are.

CONSEQUENCES

"It kinda seems fair. You break a rule, you pay for it."
- Stephanie

Just as teens want rules to make them feel more secure, they expect something to happen when they break the rules. Penalties are proof positive that their parents care what happens to them, and teens really do understand this. And as in rules, teens want consequences to make sense, to be fair. In fact, they want "logical consequences." This means that some thought is required before sentence is passed.

How to Set Consequences

BE FLEXIBLE

If teens were angels, this book wouldn't be necessary. Making mistakes is a big part of growing up and it's important to remember this periodically. In fact it is usually through their mistakes and the subsequent consequences, that teens learn best. Consider Natasha's thoughts on parental discipline:

"They're trying to protect me from all the bad in this world. But they don't understand that I have to learn on my mistakes and not on their words."

Regarding infringements, it is wise to be flexible. They may be so involved with what they're doing that they forget the time. If they miss curfew by a few minutes, is it really worth getting excited about? If they are on the phone a little too long and nobody needs it, why worry? By all means mention the fact, to show you are paying attention. But don't be too picky unless there is a good reason. As Cheyenne says:

> *"Being 10/15 minutes late doesn't mean you're unfaithful, untrustworthy. This kind of thing doesn't deserve a punishment."*

Hilary agrees when she asks that her parents:

> *"Not get as mad over stupid things like coming home a bit late or something."*

Now if the family has an airplane to catch these few minutes do become important, and a consequence would be in order.

What if the bedroom isn't cleaned to your standards? You have to decide if the difference is worth an argument. Did the kid try? Wouldn't it be better to look on the positive side? Asking these questions could help to keep the relationship on track. The kids want the rules, but they need some flexibility for small infractions.

LISTEN FIRST

When your teen comes home an hour past curfew, they usually are met with an angry blast, the result of worry and concern. There are certainly enough dangers in today's world to cause parents to worry. As we have seen in Chapter 2, emotion only makes a complex situation even more difficult. Sometimes the situation was not the teen's fault.

> Dad: "Do you know what time it is?"
>
> Jason: "Yes, but it isn't my fault."
>
> Dad: "I don't care whose fault it is, you're over an hour late. You're grounded for two weeks."
>
> Jason: "That's not fair! Why can't you listen to me for a change?"
>
> Dad: "It certainly is fair after what you've just put your Mom and me through! Get to your room before I add another week."

At this point, the teen has the choice of continuing the argument, and increasing the risk of consequences, or going to his room as ordered, totally frustrated. Let's run that scene again with Dad taking a different approach.

> Dad: "You're over an hour late. You mother and I were really worried. What happened?"
>
> Jason: "Sorry but you know how Danny's mom was picking us up? Well out on the freeway the car had a flat tire, and she didn't have the trunk key. We had to wait until a tow truck

happened to come by. There weren't any phones and she didn't want us walking around in the dark. We were lucky the truck came by when it did."

Dad: "Whew, that makes me feel better. I'll call Danny's mom tomorrow and thank her for bringing you home."

Amber writes about unfairness in her parents' consequences:

"They are unfair only when I'm late 'cause of a flat tire or the person never showed or even if the driver was drunk (so I never took the ride). When they ground me for that it's unfair. Also they don't ever wanna pick me up so they shouldn't complain if I get a ride late."

No matter what the circumstances, it is always best to listen first. Remember, the teen is home safely now so you can relax.

DISCUSS

After you have listened to your teen and decided there was a deliberate infringement of the rules, the next step is to discuss the situation. Make it brief and thorough. Clearly state what the mistake is and give your reasons for consequences. Here's Erin's suggestion:

"Just talk calmly. Don't yell or it might make the kids get mad at you again. Talk about what happened and why."

Kristina feels her parents' discipline system could be enhanced in a similar way:

"I would improve it just by giving me fair enough reasons. If the reasons are good enough, I will obey the rules."

Sarah doesn't even realize that discussion is part of the discipline process when she writes:

"My parents don't discipline us. They always talk with us about what we do wrong. I think they taught us to discipline ourselves, because if I do some things wrong, I feel guilty — after I know my parents won't approve."

It is entirely possible, as in Sarah's family, that after the discussion, no consequence is necessary. If the mistake was a simple one like forgetting what time it was, then talking about it may be enough. If it's the third time this has happened in the past few months, then discuss it, but this time tack on the penalty.

NEGOTIATE

The next step is to ask the guilty party what consequence should be administered. The results of this process are often surprising. Most of the time the teen will suggest a consequence that is more severe than any you may have had in mind. Rarely will the suggestion be too mild.

The recommendation gives you a starting point from which you can negotiate a compromise, thus giving the teen some control. This

---

WHEN DISCUSSION IS NOT ENOUGH

Logical consequences are usually necessary when:
- the offense is serious — like drinking, shoplifting or vandalizing
- the offense is deliberate — the party was so much fun that the teen didn't want to come home
- it is a repeat offense — earlier discussions had no effect

makes them a part of the discipline system. Most teens prefer this method to simply having rules and consequences imposed upon them.

Jessica recognizes the value of negotiation:

> *"I think my parents are pretty cool when it comes to rules and punishments. When it comes to punishing they always ask me what I think it should be and then we compromise."*

The Consequences

The most difficult part of the disciplinary process is thinking up an appropriate consequence. Each situation and each teenager has unique characteristics, so it is not possible to list effective consequences that will work for everyone. Here are some guidelines you can follow:

1. *Make the consequence happen quickly.* Teens soon forget the seriousness of an incident unless the consequence is immediate. It should occur within a few days.
2. *Don't carry it on for too long.* It is almost impossible to enforce a consequence for longer than a week — there are just too many things happening.
3. *Relate the consequence to the offense.* If too much time has been spent on the telephone, remove the privilege for a day or two. If money has been spent frivolously, stop the allowance for a week.
4. *Use only one consequence for each offense.* If you are really upset, there is sometimes a tendency to keep adding on consequences: for example, not allowing the teen to attend an upcoming school dance, and then removing telephone privileges.
5. *Don't relate consequences to loss of affection.* Give out the consequence, but let the teen know you still love him or her.
6. *Be consistent.* The system will fall apart if you don't hand out the consequences when the teens expect them.

How Not to Set Logical Consequences

> *"The good part about my parents discipline is that they listen, and then get mad. They don't just yell if I was right." – Crystal*

Remember that teenagers expect consequences when they have done something wrong. Mistakes are a major part of growing up, and unfortunately the best way to teach that they should not be repeated is to correct the major ones.

> *"When I do something bad they get angry but they should try to understand that teenagers experiment with different things and it's normal to get in trouble at this age." – Briana*

Virtually all teens resent grounding as a consequence. The response on this subject was overwhelming. Hearing from some of the more articulate teens should help convince you of their passionate resentment.

> *"Grounding doesn't work. It makes me more upset and I never want to go home." – Cheyenne*

> *"My parents punish me by grounding and it really does nothing to improve the way I behave. It usually causes me to give my parents attitude and when my sentence is complete I'm only going to behave worse because the freedom overwhelms me after sitting in the house bored for a month." – Linda*

> *"Don't ground your kids! This does nothing. This teaches us nothing but to sit in our room, doing nothing and when we get out, we get even more mad at our parents and we yell at them. Then they ground us again and it keeps going around in circles." – Erin*

"They used to overuse grounding, and eventually my home was only a house, a place where I did not look forward to going to. Now they use other things such as chores and even though I hate them as much as any other punishment, they don't make me feel trapped inside my house." – Robyn

The problem with grounding is usually that it goes on too long. To be effective consequences should be immediate, and connected with the mistake. Dragging them on for weeks or months is excessive and the effectiveness is replaced by resentment and anger. For an unusual viewpoint on this subject, here's what Lawrence wrote:

"My mother used to spank me with a wooden spoon or belt. I felt it was a good method of discipline. It is a lot better than being grounded."

While physical punishments for teens are never acceptable, Lawrence's preference probably comes from the desire to take the punishment as the consequence and get it over with.

The next "don't" has already been covered in the last chapter, and that is "don't lecture." Once you have determined that the teen really has made a mistake, explain why it is wrong (the teen usually knows anyway), then hand out the consequence. As Diana says, "once I get it, STOP!"

The final caution has already been covered, and that is "yelling." This blocks communication and brings harmful emotions into the situation. When asked how to improve her parents' system of rules and consequences Carey responded:

"I would improve by cutting out the yelling completely and when and if we are bad, just assign us a job or punishment."

Briana has a very good relationship with her mother, but still says:

"The only problem I have with my Mom is that she never thinks about my feelings before she flies off the handle. I think she should calm down and plan what she would like to say."

Before you decide, take a short pause, remember who is in control, then hand out the consequences. If the error is a really serious one and you are extremely upset, wait until the next day to deliver the sentence. You'll be glad you did.

WHAT NOT TO DO

- Don't use long groundings. Use short ones or not at all.
- Don't lecture. Make your point, then quit.
- Don't yell. Stay calm and under control.

CASE HISTORY

Let's run through a case history (a real one) to get a clearer picture of the consequence process.

The Scene: Mrs. Smith has just called you to say that while she and Mr. Smith were away over the weekend, your daughter Jane and two of her friends got into the Smiths' house (they knew where the key was kept), took the keys to the sports car, and drove it around town. In the process, they damaged one fender. One of the girls, worried about police involvement, told the story to her guidance counselor. The counselor advised her to tell her parents, which she did and now you are involved.

The Time: 5:30 p.m. Jane is just coming home from her piano lessons. As she opens the door and enters the house, she is met by two anxious-looking parents.

Jane: "What's the matter?"

Dad: "Mrs. Smith just called and told us a pretty strange story."

Jane: [suddenly looking scared] "What about?"

Dad: "I think you already know. She said that you girls stole their sports car on the weekend. Is this true?"

Jane: "No way. I don't know anything about it."

Time out: The seriousness of the situation, combined with the obvious lie, could readily lead to an explosion, take a deep breath, relax and continue.

Mom: "Lying will only make things worse. This is serious and you're going to need our help to straighten it out. Did you take the car?"

Jane: [looking at her feet] "Yes."

Mom: "Why? You've never done anything like this before."

Jane: "I don't know."

Mom: "Tell us what happened that night."

Jane: "We were walking past Leslie Smith's house on our way to the bus stop, when Sally said that she knew where they kept the house keys. We knew the Smiths were away for the weekend. Then Sally went and got the keys and said she was going in. Jessie and I didn't really want to but Sally called us chickens, so we finally went in."

Dad: "What did you think you were going to do?"

Jane: "I don't really know. It just seemed kind of exciting to be in someone else's house when they're not home."

Mom: "Why did you take the car?"

Jane: "That was really weird. We saw the keys hanging on a peg. I don't even remember whose idea it was. We just decided to go for a little drive. Sally didn't even know how to drive a standard. As she was backing out of the driveway, she hit a post with the front fender. It was just about dark and it didn't seem too bad, so we kept driving."

Dad: "Did you drive it?"

Jane: "Yeah. We all took turns. Then we went over to Matt's house and picked him up. After a while all our friends drove it. We kept it all weekend, parked behind Matt's house."

Dad: "This is incredible. I can't believe you would do a thing like this."

Another time out: There is no doubt that all caring parents would be almost numb with shock at this point. The effects of the first pause have now worn off so it's time to renew the calmness with a few more deep breaths. When you feel like you are about to lose control, STOP for a few moments. Regain control before moving on. Once the teen is telling the story, you have control, don't lose it by exploding now. If you find yourself getting too tense, postpone the consequences until the next day. It's best though to get it done as quickly as possible.

Mom: "How do you think we should handle this situation?"

Jane: "I guess I should get punished."

Mom: "What do you think would be fair?"

Jane: "I'll help pay for the fender out of my
        allowance, and I probably should be
        grounded for a month."

Dad: "You certainly will pay. I also think you
        should go over and apologize to the Smiths.
        I don't think a month's grounding will teach
        you anything, but you can't go to the school
        dance on Friday, and we will ask that a
        school resource policeman come and talk to
        you about what could have happened if the
        Smiths had decided to press charges."

Mom: "We understand about peer pressure, but
        please think next time before doing some-
        thing this stupid. You were very, very lucky."

Both parents give Jane a hug, and they carry on to dinner.

The key points to notice are:

a. the calmness throughout (whether they felt calm or not);
b. listening to the entire story (with a little prompting) before
   passing judgment;
c. asking for teen input on the consequences first, then adding
   and subtracting;
d. keeping the sermon short (maybe too short, but Jane already
   knows where she was wrong, so it doesn't help to draw things
   out too much); and
e. the reassuring hug at the end — she blew it, but you still love
   her.

With a little practice, disciplinary situations will not become cause
for resentment that could threaten the relationship with your teen.
Even better, you will earn your child's respect while making home a
secure place.

The development and application of a disciplinary system is vital
to teens. "Hear Me" and "Hug Me" are both important parts of this
process.

APPROPRIATE DISCIPLINE

Remember

- Teens want rules.
- They expect consequences for breaking rules.

Setting Rules

- Use family meetings.
- Get the teen's input first, then compromise.
- Determine what rules are reasonable.
- Renegotiate yearly.

Applying Consequences

- Be flexible for minor infractions.
- Listen to the entire explanation.
- Ask what the teen thinks should happen.
- Apply the consequences immediately.
- Let them know you still love them.

4

Fair Play

**❝ Let me start making some of my own
decisions over small things that aren't
going to affect my whole life. Even if I can't
make big ones, at least I have some say. ❞**
– Cheryl

4. Show FAIRNESS

Teenagers have some sort of built-in alarm that goes off whenever they perceive something unfair. What is also certain is that teens consider fairness to be a major component of good parenting. Since the teens themselves can't tell parents how they define this concept, it is necessary to analyze their complaints to find out what "fairness" really is.

After I read and listened to hundreds of concerns about parents from teens, I found that fairness breaks down into four areas:

1. being listened to;
2. being treated equally with regard to siblings;
3. being seen as an individual when it comes to abilities; and
4. parental consistency.

Let's examine each of these areas in more detail.

81

BEING LISTENED TO

When teens demand "fairness," they mean being listened to when there is a difference of opinion — hearing their side of the story. We have already discussed this in the previous chapter, but it is so important that it is worth having another look at listening from a "fairness" approach. Teens want the chance to tell their side of what went wrong or why they want to do something from start to finish, before any judgments are made. Even if the final outcome is not in their favor, they want to feel as if their viewpoint has at least been fully considered before any decisions are made. Doug certainly feels this strongly when he says:

> *"My parents and I fight over everything. My Mom seems to lack the ability to see things from my point of view. Especially when school and friends are concerned."*

Laura, although two years younger than Doug, agrees fully with him when she writes:

> *"Just because they're the parents they think they're always right and don't listen to any other points of view."*

The fact is that parents *are* usually right and if pressed most teens will agree with this. But they still want their side of things heard and some compromises made. When asked if her parents were ever unfair, Vanessa wrote:

> *"Yes, if they think one thing and I think another, they are ALWAYS right just because they're parents. Sometimes they will see things my way but a part of their opinion is always in the outcome."*

Hilary feels that her parents are unfair:

> *"When they don't listen to what I have to say before getting angry at me, when they accuse me before actually finding out the truth."*

There seems little doubt that a major component of the teenagers' idea of fairness is listening carefully to their side of the story, and considering things from their point of view. Tracey adds another component to the definition when she states:

"They always suspect the worst in me and don't even let me have the smallest leeway. I just hope one day they realize that my side of the story is actually important."

> **There seems little doubt that a major component of the teenagers' idea of fairness is listening carefully to their side of the story.**

At first glance, Tracey appears to be concerned mainly about parental listening, but there is another important element in her statement. In asking for some "leeway," she is really looking for *the freedom to make some mistakes, to learn for herself.* Listening to why she wants to do something new or different is part of the "fairness," but letting her try some of these things is even more important.

Listening, then, can also mean trying things the teens' way. It's part of giving them the freedom they want and need, to show that they really are individuals with a separate identity from their parents.

EQUAL TREATMENT

Children tend to be much more observant than most adults realize. That is certainly true when it comes to parenting methods. Another area they watch carefully is how they are treated in comparison with their brothers and sisters. At the slightest variation, teens will raise the "unfair" banner. The main issues that concern them involve rules and privileges, blame and household duties.

Rules and Privileges

Trying to be fair to all children in the family when it comes to rules and privileges is like learning to ride a bicycle. You have to be constantly adjusting your balance or you will crash. The balance involved here is that between both the ages of the teens and their sex. The problems involved can differ greatly from family to family. While one group may give the oldest considerable freedom and restrict their "baby," another family might give the younger sibling exactly the same rules as the older one. In the first family, the younger child feels unfairly restrained, whereas in the second family, the older teen feels that more freedom is his right.

Gender adds another complication. Girls often feel that their male siblings, whether older or younger, have more latitude than they do just because they are males.

The complaints in this area from teens represent one of their biggest concerns. Craig writes:

*"I am 14 and have a brother who is 15 and all the time
he gets to go to parties and stay out till 11 but I never
can because I am supposedly too young."*

In this case the age difference is so small that Craig has a good
point. When the difference is two or three years, it makes sense to
have different rules. To avoid conflict, though, the rules need to be
adjusted regularly and the reasons for them explained carefully.

Sara has several concerns on this topic:

*"My parents are always unfair when it comes to using
the phone — they always kick me off so that my sister
can use it for the rest of the night, and it's usually around
7:30 when they kick me off. My sister has a 12:30 curfew
and I have an 11:00 curfew, and if I'm late I get yelled
at, and if she's late she gets a 'Where were you? Oh okay.'
Also my sister is allowed out on school nights. I'm not
allowed out on school nights and if I am it's usually for
about an hour."*

It's obvious that Sara's family has some balancing and explaining
to do. As a ninth grade student she certainly has a strong need for the
telephone, so it would probably be best if her parents tried to make a
more even distribution. She doesn't say how much older her sister is,
but it is usually fair that the older teen have more freedom, as long as
the younger one gets the same rules when she reaches her sibling's
age. To reduce Sara's obvious resentment, her parents definitely need
to sit down with her, listen to her concerns, then explain their reasons for the rule differences. Some small adjustments might just reduce her bitterness. Amanda is at the opposite end of this problem:

*"My parents are really overprotective of me (I'm the old-
est) and they treat me like my 12-year-old sister. They
need to let me be 14 instead of staying their little baby.
It's hard to grow up when your parents don't let you."*

Here is a concern from Peter that absolutely cries out for an answer:

"My parents are letting my brother go to Europe for which they have to fork out $2200, but they won't buy me a $300 stereo."

The parents probably do have a good reason for this apparent favoritism, but Peter is not aware of it. Communications are evidently not very good in the family. Most of these example problems could be solved with communication, rather than by changing rules and privileges.

Allowances can be another topic of concern. Stephanie has been simmering for some time when she writes:

"When I was younger my brother got more allowance than me (he's two years older), but we still should have gotten at least just about the same instead of $12 (me) and $20 (bro)."

There is an infinite variety of possibilities for unfairness or perceived lack of justice within a family. As if there weren't already enough, a new one has recently been added. Where differences between the treatment of boys and girls was once expected, it is now being openly questioned. Laurel releases some of her frustrations on paper by saying:

"I hate it when you have a brother 2 years younger but he can do the stuff and more you can do now just because he's a boy. AHHHHHHHHH!"

Mandy, another ninth grade student, has another interesting story about gender differences:

"My Dad won't let my sister and I stay home for the weekend by ourselves. We don't always want to go where they go. My Mom thinks we are old enough to stay home but for some reason she won't say anything to my Dad. My

Dad says if they go away for a weekend and leave us at home that all our friends will come over and a party will occur. But my Dad doesn't understand or trust us. We won't let anyone into the house. Once my sister and I asked my Dad if we were boys would he let us stay home. He said yes. That made me mad. We asked why he said "just because".

The whole issue of staying home alone is a tricky one, but Dad has made it much trickier. It boils down to a matter of trust.

In these times it is difficult to justify stricter rules for female children. It does make sense to ensure that girls have a guaranteed ride home at night, but this could be said for boys too, as they can get into different kinds of trouble. As a general guideline, parents should allow equal privileges at equal ages, regardless of the sex of their teen.

> *As a general guideline, parents should allow equal privileges at equal ages, regardless of the sex of their teen.*

Setting rules and allowing privileges fairly for all siblings requires not only a sense of fairness, but good communication. Those renegotiating meetings discussed in the last chapter take on new importance in the light of the examples of these grievances.

Blame

Trying to determine who did what to whom in a family squabble can be a frustrating task. Siblings tend to see the problem from their own point of view, and almost always believe themselves to be in the right. Assigning the blame to one party can lead to a considerable build up of resentment. In some families, blame seems to be automatically allotted to the older teen, since it is believed that age should make him or her more responsible. Like rules and privileges, however, each family seems to have its own methods of dealing with these situations.

Here are two quotes that illustrate both the assigning of blame and the differences in how families handle the situations.

"Sometimes when they are comparing punishments to me and to my brother, I get most of the blame, seeing how I'm the oldest. – Michael

"Sometimes when my older brother kicks my butt they get more mad at me than him. They say I shouldn't tempt him and bug him when I wasn't doing anything to start with. – Kris

The unfairness of these situations is obvious when you read about them. It's different when a parent is in the middle of this type of predicament. They don't happen when you're relaxed and well rested, but when you are dead tired after a hard day at work. The result is a snap decision that may tend to favor one side. A better response would be to make a decision that stops the fight, but does not assign blame to either participant. Let's take Clint's complaint as an example:

"One time my parents and I had an argument about me pushing my sister. My parents said 'You're bigger and you shouldn't shove her,' so I said 'Then she shouldn't bug me bad enough to make me shove her.' My parents told me not to do it again so I said fine. My point is that siblings should be treated equal no matter how young they are."

Clint probably believes that treating siblings "equally" means taking his side. There is no doubt he should not have pushed his sister. On the other hand, there is also little question that younger children can pester their older siblings when they want attention. A better response from Clint's parents would have been to caution both sides about their behavior, and possibly throw in a short commercial about both kids being in the same family.

Graeme, who lists his family as being even more important than his girlfriend, still has a problem with his mom because he says:

"My most continuous argument with my Mom is about me and my sister. For instance, my sister will swear or insult me and my Mom doesn't notice or seem to care. If I swear or insult her, I get in trouble. Then we fight even more."

This problem appears to be one of Mom protecting the female. Overprotection of girls can work against them, but in this situation it works for them and against the boy. In today's society, equal treatment for the sexes works much better. (It probably always did.)

When siblings disagree, parents need to listen carefully to both sides of the story, then deal with each problem individually. Since it takes two to have a disagreement, there is probably some fault on both sides. While it is hard to be patient enough to listen to both sides when you are tired, it pays dividends when your teens perceive you to be acting fairly.

Household Chores

A third area where siblings want to be treated equally is in the assigning of household responsibilities. Again both the age of the teen and their sex is often a factor in what is seen as unfairness. Consider Valerie's response when asked if her parents were ever unfair:

"Yes. To each of us kids. I usually get stuck with most of the work and the others just sit around watching TV and my parents don't do anything about it. "

Derek has a similar problem:

"Yes, they always come down harder on me than my sister. She never has to do anything."

Sometimes a problem results because parents believe that older children should have more responsibilities. In fact this philosophy makes good sense. Most teens would probably agree with it, as long as the idea behind the unequal distribution is carefully explained to them, and as long as the younger ones have some chores to do, no matter how menial in comparison. There are times, however, when the older child definitely needs to have duties re-evaluated. Kristin is a good example of this type of situation:

> *"My Dad wasn't around a lot since my parents divorced about five years ago so it was just my Mom and I and my younger sister and brother so I had to take on a lot of responsibilities and my Mom and I argued about that a lot, about how often I baby-sat my siblings and about how my responsibilities conflicted with my personal freedoms and privacy."*

A single mom does need to count on her oldest daughter (or oldest son) to help out. Again, though, a re-evaluation of these responsibilities is necessary periodically, so that a balance is achieved between the freedom the teen needs and the help the mother requires. Since most teens have difficulty talking to their parents about topics such as rules and responsibilities, it is up to the parent to sit down with them once a year to see if adjustments are required.

One parental habit that upsets teens is to compare them to others, especially with regard to schoolwork. One last quote should complete this picture. Try to imagine how you would handle Colleen's concern:

> *"My sister gets away with everything just cuz she's not doing so well in school. She gets to skip doing all her chores to 'study' (yeah right) and I end up doing all her chores as well as mine. Then when I make a comment or complain about it (rightfully so) I get the lecture and/ or grounded!"*

Colleen's own solution is:

> *"Be fair! Ask us how we feel before making decisions! Be normal when you talk to us."*

Hopefully, better communication was your solution to the problem as well. While relieving the weaker student from chores in order to let her study might be a valid short-term solution (as long as she was actually using the time to study), it is definitely not fair for the older sister to have to pick up the leftover tasks. The chores could either be moved to the weekend when the sister had more time, or if a daily task like dishwashing was involved, it could be exchanged for a weekly one.

INDIVIDUAL ABILITIES

Fairness, to teens, is often the recognition that each one is a unique individual with his or her own strengths and weaknesses.

As soon as the parent compares their teen with one more successful in sports or music, sparks fly. To protect teens' self-esteem, try to assess their abilities as accurately as possible and motivate them in more positive ways than trying to get them to compete.

The assessment process is a difficult one. Every parent wants their teen to be successful — to go to university, to play in the NHL, to have a high-profile profession. Unfortunately they are not all capable of these lofty goals. If you are paying attention, though, the information you need to accurately appraise your teen's abilities, and to (help) set goals accordingly, is abundantly available. Parent-teacher interviews over the years, going to games, and attending recitals, will show you how your child compares to his or her contemporaries. Then set expectations *for each child* accordingly. Teaching them to set realistic goals and to do the best they can is far more effective than trying to set them into competition with a cousin or brother.

> *Fairness, to teens, is often the recognition that each one is a unique individual with his or her own strengths and weaknesses.*

"We always fight about schoolwork. I get slightly above average to average grades. My Mom especially doesn't

understand that not everyone is a Doogie Howser! She
should be proud of me when I get 80 on a test instead
of saying I should go study so I can do better next
time." – Amanda

There is also another side to this coin. Often when one child in
the family has less ability than another, parents overcompensate. In
trying hard to prop up the self-esteem of the poor student or less talented sibling, parents may appear to neglect the accomplishments of
the talented teen. Once again, a delicate balancing act is required as
even talented children need praise and encouragement. Sandy illustrates this point clearly:

"She also favors my little brother. For example, he doesn't
get as good marks as me. He even failed one major sub-
ject. My lowest mark was 75% and my overall average
85.7% and she kept praising him for his work. All she
said to me was 'good work'. She's not exactly what you'd
call the fairest mother in the world even though I still
love her."

When this type of unfairness happens, it may be because the parents either don't want the less talented child to feel bad or because
they're trying to avoid giving the more talented one a swollen head.
Good thoughts, but the strategy doesn't work well. Instead, praise
the talented one when the less talented sibling is not present. Discuss
with all of your children the difference in their abilities, how you love
them all equally, and how you have different expectations for each
child. This will probably have to be done more than once — kids
have short memories at times (especially when you ask them to clean
their bedroom).

Punishing for Poor Marks

Since the subject of school grades has come up, this is as good a time
as any to suggest that punishment not be used to try to improve grades.

It almost never works, and develops tremendous resentment. This quote from Kristina illustrates the point:

> *"When I get punished, I get punished harsh. If my marks slip from 80% to 74%, they'll ground me and I can do nothing until my marks are sky high. I know they want me to get a decent education, but why take things overboard?"*

If grades slip there is usually a reason — the teen doesn't understand the work, there is conflict with the teacher, the teen is rebelling against something at home, etc. It is far more effective to try to find the answer, then work with the teen and the teachers to improve, than it is to just drop a punishment on them and expect results. A positive approach is always preferred to a negative one.

> **A positive approach is always preferred to a negative one.**

PARENTAL CONSISTENCY

The final instance where teens are prone to scream "That's not fair!" is when parents act in an inconsistent manner. This can happen in disciplinary situations (as was discussed in Chapter 3) but it can also be due to parents' stress and fatigue. There is not always a preventive measure for these times — they happen suddenly and without warning. Often, the only answer is a simple apology. Erica's story is funny to her now, but it certainly wasn't at the time:

> *"When we argue it's usually not the minuscule problem we're arguing about, it's always a fight about how controlling my Dad is. One time it was my Mom though and I walked in after school to discover my Mom had come home early to relieve herself of the pressures of work and the instant she saw me she said 'Take your*

*shoes off and put them in the garage.' The funny thing
was, my shoes were already off. Then when I told her
that she said irritably 'Don't talk back to me, I'm sick
of you, get to your room.' So I started up the stairs,
when I was halfway up she yelled 'Get back down here,
don't walk away from me when I'm talking to you.' So
I came back down, the instant I got off the stairs she
yelled 'Get to your room, I've had it up to here with you.'
So I went back up the stairs and she told me not to walk
away from her when she's talking to me. Finally after
3 more rounds she got so frustrated she gave up and
left. It's a good thing she did cause I was getting tired."*

Mom was already stressed out before Erica got home and as often happens, the frustration was taken out on the nearest person, instead of dealing with the real cause of the stress. Once rested, mom probably felt pretty sheepish about the episode.

Don't ignore such unprovoked outbursts. Teens understand stress vaguely, if at all. They tend to take these occurrences very personally, and even blame themselves for them. An apology or explanation is vital to your relationship, especially if it happens often. We are all human and, in this hurry-up world, can get tense easily. Teens are definitely capable of understanding this, if it is explained to them as soon as rationality returns.

To close this chapter, here is Ed's story:

*"My mother argues about everything. One day I was
in my room and she comes in with an empty shampoo
bottle. She starts accusing me that I used all her shampoo that she bought a few days ago. The problem was
that it's for permed and damaged hair and I don't have
either one of those so that would wreck my hair. Besides I have my own shampoo. But she keeps yelling at
me saying I'm just like my father and she tells me what
a bad husband he was. Even though that's got nothing*

to do with me. And finally I get so p—ed off I just leave until night time."

The tendency to bring unrelated sore points into an argument is quite common. It is usually done under the influence of strong emotions in an attempt to hurt the other party. It's hard for adults to understand how this happens, and virtually impossible for teens.

Fairness is to teens like art is to many of us: we don't know much about the reasons behind it, but we know what we like. Teens have a strong need for fairness in their lives.

Listening, to teen concerns and to their side of the story, is a key element in being fair. Again the phrase "Hear Me" reminds us of this.

HOW TO BE FAIR TO TEENS

- Listen to the teen's side of the story before reacting.
- Keep rules, privileges and chores balanced among siblings.
- Let the teens know you understand their differences.
- Be consistent.

5

Trust Me

*No, my parents don't trust me. My
life is a living hell most of the time.*
- Lisa

5. Demonstrate TRUST

Teenagers are a study in contrasts. On the one hand they need rules
and consequences to feel secure; on the other hand they require ever
increasing amounts of freedom to create an identity for themselves.

The knowledge that their parents trust them is vital to teenagers
because of the close relationship between trust and independence.
The feeling of freedom trust gives comes from several sources.

One is the knowledge that the teen is not being checked on, that
there are no strings between the parents and what the teen is doing.
Too many questions before going to the mall, for example, give teens
a stifled feeling which can stay with them the entire time they are away
from home.

Another source of feeling trusted, and therefore independent, is
being able to make decisions and having those decisions respected.
The ability to make a decision to buy a particular CD or to see a movie
that their parents would not want to see (or even would not want them
to see) makes them feel separate from the people who have decided

things for them for so long. This separateness is an important feeling for teens, so important that if they don't get it they will usually rebel. A solid foundation of trust between parent and teen will head off any such thoughts of rebelling. There is no need to assert your independence if your parents are already giving it to you.

The problem for parents is that they are the ones who have to sit home and worry when their child is out doing something new. Who knows what kinds of things are happening at that party? Will he or she be tempted to do something dumb at the rock concert? The letting go process is extremely difficult for most parents because it means taking chances that something could go wrong. Unfortunately the process of growing up continues whether parents want it to or not. For maturity to develop, teens need the rope to be let out in gradually increasing lengths — partly by easing off on the rules, and partly by allowing teens to decide things for themselves. It is a scary but rewarding process when everything works out.

BUILDING TRUST

Tell Them

Amazingly, just telling your teen that you trust them has a powerful effect. Unless your actions are opposite to your words, teens will accept what you say at face value and respond accordingly. This is certainly true in Marcie's case:

> *"I know they trust me because they come right out and tell me. There's no guessing if you keep everything open."*

Even though actions speak louder than words, in the case of trust words seem to be almost as effective. If there is a good relationship between parents and teens, telling them is often enough because they will then not want to let their parents down.

Sincerity is important to this trust. Consider Brendon's thoughts on whether his parents trust him:

"Most of the time, yes. My mother is always telling me that she lets me do certain things because she 'trusts' me. She tells me that the only reason that she lets me hang around with certain friends is because she trusts me. But all this tells me is that she doesn't really trust my friends or even my choice of friends."

Despite the fact that the trust has been stated, the implication that Brendon has not made good decisions in the choice of friends has made him feel he is not fully trusted after all. If you are going to say it, make sure you mean it.

Keep Questions to a Minimum

"They shouldn't be so nosy. I'm sick of them asking me about every single thing that happens in my life. Maybe I don't want to tell them. Do parents really need to know everything?" - Erica

Let's make one thing clear right now. Parents have a right to have a certain amount of information before allowing their teen to go somewhere or do something, and most teenagers understand this. If too much information is demanded, this tells teens they are still not capable of handling themselves on their own.

"I can tell my parents trust me because they will always let me go places and do things with my friends, as long as I let them know where I'm at, who I'm with and when I'll be back." - Sally

Some teens might complain that even these "big three" questions Sally mentioned are too much, but most understand the need for them. Problems will develop when the "big three" turn into the "frustrating five" or even the "terrible ten."

How do teens feel when the questioning is overdone? Rachel's comments on whether her parents trust her are:

"No, because it doesn't matter where I'm going they still want to know every single detail of what's going on."

Derek agrees:

"Sometimes I can tell when they don't trust me because they question me and that makes me angry because I think that they think I'm a liar."

Rather than the parents asking the big three each time, teach the teen to volunteer this information. A short discussion explaining why parents need to know these things, and requesting that the information be given before going out anywhere, will keep each parting from becoming a minor inquisition. Instead of, "Where are you going?" "Who with?" and "When will you be home? it would be, "Bye Mom, I'm going to the mall with Sheri. I'll be home around 4:00."

As teens get older and start staying out later at night, a fourth piece of information should be volunteered — how the teen will get home. If the arrangements are not satisfactory, volunteer to pick him up yourself.

Making Decisions

Another way of showing you trust your teens is allowing them to make decisions on issues that affect them. Within the house rules, they should be allowed to make most of their own decisions. Trust comes in accepting that these decisions will be good ones.

Stephanie, when asked if she was trusted, gave some examples of decisions she is allowed to make:

"Yes. They let me decide my bedtime. They trust me with the friend that I hang out with. They don't tell me how to spend my money. They trust that I will do my school-work and have it done on time."

Courtney shows how important making her own choices is to her:

"When I ask to go out somewhere with my friends and they agree then it gives me a feeling of trust. This helps me also to be truthful. If I lie I feel guilty, and the more I'm trusted the more I will continue to be truthful."

On such topics as buying CDs or what to do on Saturday afternoon, it is easy to let your teen make the decision. The consequences of making a bad choice are minimal. Even Dave's decisions, although costly, did not have any long-term effects:

"I bought lots of (baseball) cards with my paper route money and didn't tell my parents. After about five months I spent close to $1,000. Then my parents wanted to look at my bank book to see how much money I had. As it turns out I had $2.60. They had a hairy. To this day and forward I feel like a fool because I could have had an extra $1,000."

Since Dave was the only loser, and since he obviously learned from the mistake, his parents would not need to take any action beyond a short discussion of the value of money.

Some teen decisions can have more serious consequences. Example: to attend a party where there is a strong chance that drugs or alcohol will be present. The parents have to trust that the teen will not decide to indulge. If the relationship is sound, you won't have to worry. Jana is quite clear on this very issue:

"They let me make my own choices instead of making them for me. I'm allowed to pretty much go where I want just as long as I act responsibly and do what they say. If I don't lie about my plans and tell them the truth, like if people are drinking where I'm going, it shows I'm trustworthy so they trust me back."

If teens truly believe their parents trust them, the decisions they make will be good ones. They will not want to let their parents down.

*"The major fight I can remember happened last year. I
told my Mom that I was old enough to do what I wanted
and to make my own decisions and she couldn't tell me
what to do. We ended up arguing about it for a couple of
hours and the result was me not speaking to her for about
a month." - Jaime*

Trust First

In order for trust to develop, somebody has to start trusting. The teens
can't do much until they get opportunities to show they can be relied
on to go where they say they're going and
do what they say they are going to do.
The onus is on the parent to start this
process rolling. Trust should continue
until there is clear reason for not trusting. Lindsay says exactly this:

> **Trust should
> continue until
> there is clear reason
> for not trusting.**

*"I don't think that parents should
let kids stay out all night, and drink, and steal and not
know where they are at 3 a.m., but they should let them
make some of their own decisions, and trust them a bit.
Parents say you have to gain trust before you can do this
or that. But you can't show that you're trustworthy without privileges."*

"Trusting first" is made up of:
1. letting teens make their own decisions;
2. not asking too many questions immediately before the event
   and right after they return;
3. not checking up on them while they're away.

As long as teens come home at the agreed-on time and no trouble
has been reported, parents have to believe that they went where they
said they would, and with whom they said they were going. This is
trust — and it definitely can be scary.

If it's any consolation, freedom can be just as frightening for the teen. Kristin says:

> *"The thing that is most important to me right now is being independent, especially proving to myself that I am or can be independent. It's really scary because in less than three years I will have to go out and face a world I really don't know very much about. And I don't know if I'll be ready for it."*

How can anyone learn to live in the real world unless they get some practice? The only way is to be given freedom through trust, in gradually increasing doses. Doug's thoughts are right on topic:

> *"The perfect parents are the ones who are honest, fair, kind, and a good example for their children to follow. Another thing is that they should let us have our own way of doing things and let us have the right amount of freedom at the right time."*

Giving "the right amount of freedom at the right time" is a tall order. The "right" amounts will vary from teen to teen, depending on maturity level. Once again the key is communication. If teenagers are afraid to ask, parents won't know that they are ready for more freedom. If communications within the family are good, and your teen asks for more privileges, he or she is probably ready for them. The only way to find out is to try. If the request is clearly outrageous, like a 12-year-old asking to go to a midnight movie, then obviously a refusal with an explanation is in order. Otherwise, try letting out the rope. You will not likely be disappointed.

The final part of the trusting process is that once parents have granted permission for their teen to go out, assume that is where the teen is unless there is clear information to the contrary. Checking up is incredibly destructive to trust. No matter how stealthily it is done, the teen will eventually find out. You either trust them or you don't.

There is nothing in between. Here is a true story which illustrates my point.

> Chris, a carefully sheltered ninth grade girl, was getting very interested in the opposite sex, but Mom was keeping the reins pretty tight. One Friday night Chris agreed to meet a young lad at the local variety store at 9:00 p.m. Unfortunately she was scheduled to babysit her 11-year-old brother that night. Shortly after her parents left she told her brother that she was going out to walk the dog, and left. Minutes later her parents returned to pick up some forgotten article and asked where Chris was. The brother told them about walking the dog. Unfortunately the dog chose that moment to enter the room. Chris, in her excitement, had forgotten to take him.
>
> The result was a tremendous row that reached the school counselor's ears on Monday. Through counseling, Chris's parents realized she needed more freedom, and Chris promised to obey all rules in the future.
>
> Two weeks later Chris asked to go to a mixed party at a fellow student's house. Her parents reluctantly agreed, with the proviso that she be home by 11:00 p.m. Waiting until that time was too much for mother, however, and she arrived at the scene at 10:30. The parents were upstairs and the party was downstairs in the recreation room. Mother rushed down, barged into the darkened room and yelled for Chris. The result was pandemonium.

While nothing except cuddling was going on, the resulting embarrassment and anger strained even that counselor's skills the following Monday.

There are two practical lessons in these two anecdotes. One, if no freedom is given, teens will eventually rebel by sneaking around, and two, once some freedom is allowed, don't check up without due cause.

Believe Their Explanations

Occasionally, teens appear to have broken their trust. Perhaps a sibling, or another parent, makes a comment indicating the teen did not really do what she said she was going to do. Or maybe he came home unusually late from school. Believe the teen until you have definite proof to the contrary. Veronica has a typical example:

> *"My parents are unfair sometimes, like when I came home late because I was at my friend's house doing my projects. They think I'm lying and don't believe me, then they ground me for something I didn't do. Parents should be able to trust their kids if they love them."*

Tim is especially outspoken on this subject:

> *"Whatever I tell them they will always question it. They don't even believe me when I tell them what I had for lunch. If I do come home and tell them marks they don't even believe that so I don't tell them anything because they won't believe me anyway."*

His solution?

> *"Even if you don't believe them you should still act as if you do because there's nothing that makes me madder than if you're telling the truth and no one will believe you. Your kids will trust you more and will tell you more."*

THE TRUSTING PROCESS

- Tell them you trust them.
- Let the teens make appropriate decisions.
- Don't ask too many questions.
- Don't check up on them.

The dilemma of wanting to believe and not being able to can be the result of reading the newspapers and seeing all the things that can go wrong. Other parents have had bad experiences with their older children, and keep a tighter rein on their younger ones. No matter what the reasons, it is always best to take their word at face value unless you have irrefutable proof to the contrary. Nadine's story provides a giant test in the practice of "believing first."

> *"I was out one night with a friend and his car broke down. I called but no one picked up the phone. We ended up spending the night at his friend's (I slept on the couch, him on the floor). When I got home the next day she exploded cuz I got home at 6:00 a.m. We explained what happened and she grounded me for two months and totally doesn't trust me now, even though I did call, she won't believe me."*

There is little doubt that this story is true as Nadine was mainly venting on paper, knowing that the information would not get back to her mother. Usually when a teen misses a curfew, the parents are still awake waiting for the phone to ring. Unfortunately Nadine's mother wasn't, and therefore was not in a position to verify the story. Nadine doesn't say if she had permission to be out with her friend in the car, but she probably had or she would not be so outraged at the ruling her mother made. The whole situation is mostly just bad luck and should probably be treated as such.

In this example we have the advantage of knowing the facts and being objective about them. Most parents faced with this kind of story would have trouble believing it, and rightly so. It's a lot to ask. In the face of no evidence to the contrary, it is indeed best to believe. If similar situations keep occurring, that is a different story.

There will more than likely be times when you are asked to accept your teen's word for something similar, and it will pay off in maintaining a trusting relationship.

WHEN TRUST IS BROKEN

Everyone makes mistakes and teens are particularly prone to them. Curfews will be missed through thoughtlessness. Peer pressure will tempt a teen to do something forbidden. How the parent handles these breaches of trust is vital to whether or not the trust continues.

Keep in mind that when you catch your teen breaking the faith, the teen has not done this *to you*. It has been done out of the excitement of doing something forbidden, out of lack of thought, or even out of fear of disappointing friends. In short, it is a mistake, so try not to take it personally.

Treat the error in isolation. In other words, don't bring up a list of the teen's past mistakes and try to form them into a pattern. There usually isn't one. Each one has its own separate set of circumstances. If mistakes are happening on a regular basis, then counseling should be sought. Otherwise, consider the breach for what it is, a human error.

But this does not mean parents should not do anything when trust is broken. Consequences (following the guidelines in Chapter 3) are definitely in order. First, what *not* to do.

The Scene: Your daughter, Clare, is normally not allowed out on school nights, but you have made an exception this once because you were told that an important project was due the next day. You gave Clare permission to go over to Louise's house as long as she was home by 10:00 p.m. On a whim, you and your wife decide to go over to the local mall for an ice-cream cone. The first person you see there is Clare, with a teen-aged boy:

Dad: "What are you doing here? You're sup-
        posed to be at Louise's."

Clare: "Ah...well... we just popped over for a few
        minutes for an ice cream."

Dad: "Well then where's Louise?"

Clare: "She didn't want to come."

Dad: "Don't lie to me. You never planned to
        work on any project, you came here to
        meet this delinquent."

Mom: "How can you do this to us? We trusted
        you."

Clare: "Just listen a minute..."

Dad: "Forget that. Last month you were an hour
        late getting home. Your marks are terrible.
        What's happening to you?"

Clare: "Nothing. Will you just listen?"

Dad: "We've done all the listening we're going
        to do. You're grounded — one month for
        sneaking out and one month for lying. Get
        in the car."

Pretty heavy stuff. The first thing to note is that a clear breach of trust has taken place. There is no way that Clare can or should escape consequences for her error. However, both dad and mom are doing things the hard way, making the situation more difficult . Mom is using a "guilt trip" approach that is quite unfair. Clare is not trying to do anything to them, she just wants to be with her boyfriend. Dad is not only not willing to listen, he is dragging in unrelated events, making Clare out to be more badly behaved than she really is.

Parents don't do this because they are cruel or unreasonable. Rather, it seems to be a way of justifying consequences, or comes from a fear that a pattern might be developing, so better mention it now. Whatever the reason, unless there is a clear relationship between events, it is not fair to bring up old mistakes in light of new ones.

A final hint before we replay the scene. To handle the situation well, the parents should have taken their daughter home before dealing with her. It is an extra penalty to embarrass a teen in front of her peers, and can only add resentment. By waiting until the family gets home, everyone has a chance to catch their breath, no one is embarrassed.

Now let's do that scene again.

Dad: "What are you doing here? You're supposed to be at Louise's."

Clare: "Ah...well... we just popped over for a few minutes for an ice cream."

Dad: "Well then where's Louise?"

Clare: "She didn't want to come."

Dad: "I think we'd better go home and discuss this situation. Say goodbye to your friend and get into the car."

At home, after a silent car ride:

Dad: "Now suppose you tell me what happened."

Clare: "Well, Jamie asked me to meet him tonight, and I really like him, so I made up that story about Louise's.

Dad: "Why didn't you tell him that you're not allowed out on week nights?"

Clare: "I don't know. I guess I just didn't want him to think that I'm a baby or something."

Dad: "Do you disagree with the rule? It's there because we think your schoolwork comes first."

Clare: "Well, yeah...I guess so. I just didn't think about that."

Dad: "What do you think your punishment should be?"

Clare: "I don't know. Maybe grounding?"

Dad: "OK. You can't go out at all this weekend, and you'll have to help your mother with the grocery shopping. And by the way, please don't try to lie to us in the future. It just makes things worse in the long run. Now off to your room and get your homework done."

There you have it. Another triumph for the ideal parent. It's heartbreaking when your child deceives you, but stay calm — it pays off. Clare knew she was wrong. Why make anything more out of it? Realizing that their parents are disappointed in them is almost punishment enough, so a short, sharp penance accompanied by a brief lecture should suffice. If a pattern of lying and sneaking around develops, it's time to examine both your communication system and your rules. Something has definitely gone wrong in the relationship, and counseling help may be required to straighten it out.

Lying

Bill Cosby (who has an earned doctorate in Educational Psychology) starts off one of his monologues with the statement "All kids are liars." Despite the fact that all children lie sometimes, most parents take it personally when they do. Their reactions on detecting a lie vary from disappointment that their child would do this to them, to intense anger.

The first step in dealing with lying is to understand that it's a natural reaction of teens, to either avoid punishment, or to be able to do something they know their parents won't allow. Understanding these reasons means you do not have to take lying personally. Instead, parents need to examine what caused the lying and find a solution. This is not to say that you must ever accept it. Just don't get upset when it happens. Deal with the reason for it rationally, just as you would for any other mistake.

Since lying starts at a very young age, teach your kids that the truth, no matter how ugly, is always preferable to a lie. This message should be continued whenever necessary throughout the teen years. Usually, if your kids can talk to you and can trust you to be fair, they won't lie. In Clare's case, it happened under a rare circumstance, one she had not encountered before — peer pressure. Once things settled down after the incident, her parents should have talked to her about how to handle peer pressure in the future.

Only when there are serious problems in a family does lying become a habit. If rules are too strict, teens will lie to get around them. If consequences are too harsh, or if they are usually accompanied by scenes of anger and yelling, teens will lie to avoid them. If parents don't approve of their teen's friends, the adolescent will say she is with other kids.

Take lying as a *symptom* of problems, not as the problem itself. Understand why it happens and deal with it.

REBUILDING TRUST

Occasionally, an incident occurs in a family that is so serious or so scary, it can't be dealt with quickly, then forgotten. Instead, its memory lingers in parents' minds and reappears every time the teen goes out. Examples of this would be if your son was caught shoplifting or brought home by the police for stealing hood ornaments. Or perhaps something like what Kari describes:

"I came home liquored out of my mind one night and got busted by my Mom. Now she thinks I'm an alcoholic. I can't go anywhere without her asking if there are going to be drugs or booze there."

Is there any wonder Kari's mom is concerned? How should parents handle these types of behavior? First, deal with the incident itself. Discipline is required for the breach of rules, or for the criminal act, so follow the guidelines for setting consequences discussed in Chapter 3: stay calm, listen to the explanation, stay calm some more, ask about a penalty, and so on (naturally the consequences will be more severe than usual.)

Next, let the teen know that this is an abnormally serious incident, and cannot just be forgotten. Tell him or her that the trust between you has been broken, and will need some time to heal. Decide between you on a probationary period. This will depend on the problem, but should normally be between six weeks and six months. During this period, you have the right to be less trusting than usual — in other words to check on your teen.

> **The bond of trust between parent and teen is a key element of the relationship.**

If your teen says she is going over to Sally's house during this probationary period, you have the right to call and make sure she is there. Perhaps the curfew time can be earlier during this probation. Make sure your teen is clear on rules for this probationary period, just as you would for a consequence.

When the probationary period is over, go back to your original system. If there is no repeat, don't ever mention this incident again. It's over. You will still remember it every time the teen goes out, but keep silent. Trust has to be rebuilt, and cannot be if you keep bringing up the past. Usually, there will be no repeat incidents, and the crisis will be over.

The bond of trust between parent and teen is a key element of the relationship. It can be strained and sometimes even temporarily broken, but no matter how much work it takes, it should never be lost. But there are those times that are a trial for most parents.

THOSE FIRST MIXED PARTIES

Whenever the subject of trust comes up, so does the question as to whether parents should be calling the parents of the teen having the party to check (1) if there will be parental supervision, and (2) on such details as timing, dress, etc. The answer is "yes" and "no." A definite "yes" for the pre-teen years, when mixed parties are new. You have the right to check these points. This is mainly in the sixth and seventh grades, but if the teen is new to the school, or has new friends, perhaps the eighth grade as well. Beyond this point it is better to accept the teen's word that all is well and not call. As their need for independence grows, your rope needs to be let out. It's time to "Trust Me."

WHEN TRUST IS BROKEN

- Listen to the explanation.
- Don't embarrass the teen in front of friends.
- Don't drag in unrelated errors from the past.
- Keep lectures down to a sentence.
- If you are too upset to deal with the issue, wait until the next day.
- Hand out the consequences quickly.
- Allow trust to be rebuilt.

6

Respect Me

❝ I can talk to my parents because they
talk to me as if I'm an equal (usually).
They listen to me and they give *advice*
as best as they can. They don't usually
tell me what to do about something. ❞
– *Melanie*

6. Give RESPECT more freely

Respect for teens is not a separate topic, but a subset of the concepts already discussed.

Respect starts with the philosophy that teens are growing up and need to be treated differently than they were as children. Respect involves the idea that instead of "kids" we now have "young adults" who are maturing. These young adults no longer accept everything at face value. Due to increased access to information and more knowledge of adult issues, they develop ideas of their own. They are impatient when parents restrict them from trying out these ideas. They need *reasons* for parental decisions that once went unquestioned, and argue or rebel when no reasons are given. Hormonal changes bring about new emotions, and they want to explore these. In short, they are becoming separate, thinking and feeling individuals.

Individuals need to have their ideas, opinions and dreams listened to without being put down. They need to be allowed to make decisions and have their choices respected. Finally, they need to be understood as having feelings different from those of their parents. Communication, trust and understanding have already been discussed in some detail. A closer look at each will show how "respect" is an integral part of each one.

RESPECT AND COMMUNICATION

Ideas

A fundamental way of allowing your teen to grow and mature is to *really listen* to them and give consideration to their ideas.

Often when teens are talking, parents are either not listening or only partly tuned in. Unfortunately, some parents don't listen at all because they don't believe their teen is capable of serious thought. Mark says:

> *"I don't think my parents respect my ideas because they think that I am only a kid and they think my ideas are stupid."*

Nancy has a slightly different reason for not being listened to:

> *"Sometimes they don't listen because I'm the youngest and they think I don't know anything."*

Other parents make an attempt at listening, but don't focus. Rachel is obviously frustrated at the way her parents listen to her:

> *"In my opinion, to show that you are really interested in what your child has to say you should stop everything. Don't put dishes away or slice carrots. Look at your kid and focus on what they are saying — otherwise you look preoccupied and uninterested."*

The first step in respecting teens' ideas, then, is to actually listen to them all the way through. The next step is to give these ideas some consideration. If they have merit, and are allowed even in part, it gives the teen a tremendous sense of satis-faction. They feel grown-up and a real part of the family, which is a neces-sary and desirable feeling, especially at this stage of their lives.

> *Just having their ideas seriously considered is enough for most teens.*

Jamie does not get this feeling:

> *"Usually instead of even listening to what I say they just start laughing. That makes me madder than anything. Sometimes they listen to me but they usually have other ideas and mine get ruled out."*

Kari's parents have a more practical approach:

> *"My parents will always believe and respect any idea or opinion that I throw at them, as long as it is under the conditions that it isn't forced on them, doesn't hurt me or them, and it's reasonable and possibly helpful."*

Kari's parents consider her ideas and judge them on their merits. If her ideas meet her parents' criteria as stated above, they are ap-proved. Simply having their ideas seriously considered is enough for most teens. This tells them their parents recognize that they do know some things, and that their ability to think is respected.

If you have been wondering throughout this discussion what kind of ideas we are talking about, let's examine one.

Ted's parents had been considering the purchase of a new sound system for several months. Throughout this time they had been collecting brochures and pamphlets in order to get the best system for their money. Ted found this information interesting and read it avidly. Finally his parents made their decision and bought a sophisticated (and expensive) system.

While they had researched the purchase carefully, Ted's parents had given little thought to where they would install the system in their home. When it arrived, they discovered it did not fit comfortably into the living room, due to the location of the windows. So they set it up in the loft, a small room overlooking the living room.

When Ted saw the setup he knew there was a problem with it, and immediately tackled his parents:

Ted: "Dad, the way you set up the new sound system isn't very good."

Dad: [slightly on the defensive] "Why not?"

Ted: "The speakers are too close together to get good stereo sound. Also, having the speakers in the loft means that the sound won't be very clear unless you're actually sitting up there."

Dad: "What do you mean? We can hear it fine from down here."

Ted: "You can hear it, but you aren't getting the full benefit of really good equipment. Why buy equipment if you aren't able to use its capabilities?"

Dad: "Listen, the system isn't for you it's for us. What do you know about sound systems anyway — you're only in the ninth grade. Just drop the subject."

If Ted actually has an idea of how to get the best out of their new sound system, Dad will never hear it. The result of this exchange is that Ted is left feeling hurt and frustrated. Dad is denying his knowledge and thinking capabilities and treating him as if he were still a young child. A better way of dealing with the situation follows. Let's take it from where Ted points out the futility of buying a first-rate system and not maximizing its sound potential.

Ted: "You can hear it, but you aren't getting the full benefit of really good equipment. Why buy top of the line equipment if you aren't able to use its capabilities?"

Dad: "Well, you may have a point, but the unit doesn't fit in the living room because of the windows."

Ted: "OK, but you don't have to have the whole unit in the living room. You could leave the cabinet in the loft, but put the speakers in the living room. Then the sound would be much clearer."

Dad: "Then you'd have wires running every-where. Your mother would never go for that."

Ted: "You could run the wires through the heating ducts, then tuck them under the baseboards. The warm air wouldn't hurt the wires, and you wouldn't even know they were there."

Dad: "You might have something there. Let's take a look at the way those ducts run and see if we could make it work. Good thinking."

The idea might not work, but by considering its feasibility, Dad is giving Ted credit for his knowledge and treating him as a contributing family member. This gives Ted a sense of identity and worth that does not develop when teens are treated like kids.

No matter how fantastic the idea, it is important to listen carefully, give it some consideration, then discuss the merits and drawbacks.

"The one thing that bothers me most about my parents is when they can't have a mature discussion, like when

they use phrases like 'Because I said so ...' or especially when they threaten me and don't give me credit for having a brain. Such as when they threaten the things most important to me, like 'If you don't do better in school hockey's over for you'. I mean I love hockey and when they threaten to do that it hurts me and only makes me madder. It solves nothing." – Raymond

Opinions

Teens have enough general knowledge to form opinions on a wide variety of subjects — a solution to the country's financial woes, an opinion on educational reform, a theory as to who will win the next election. Because they have access to the information but rarely the practical experience, these opinions may not be profound but they are always worth discussing. Brendon has excellent advice on the subject:

"Just let your child know that you are considering his/ her opinion. Don't just shoot it down by saying something like 'Why would we do that?' or 'That would never work'. Say something positive about their opinions and build from there."

The maturity shown by Brendon in this statement reinforces its content. If teens can make observations this sensible, then their opinions on other topics could be equally logical. Christine is pleased with her parents' approach to this issue. She feels that her parents do respect her opinions because she writes:

"Yes, because they don't treat me like a little baby. They treat me more like an adult and they listen to what I say without picking it apart by saying 'You can't be serious', or by correcting my grammar."

Teens are not always logical and sensible. It is certainly reasonable for parents to argue with and discuss teens' viewpoints, and not accept everything they say. It's *fair consideration of the opinion* that is the teen's necessity. Often teens will purposely take a side opposite from their parents, such as opting for the opposite political party to assert their independence. Rather than dismissing these contrary thoughts, discuss and debate them. Teens will feel important and valued and who knows, *you* may learn something.

Dreams and Goals

If you ask a seven-year-old boy what he wants to be when he grows up, he will say "a police officer" or "a firefighter," or some other action-oriented career. Since times are changing fast young girls may be stating similar career goals. In the past they might have said "dancer" or "nurse."

If teens have any idea at all about what they want to do with their lives, it will usually be to become a high-profile or highly-paid professional such as a doctor or lawyer. Veterinarian and marine biologist are often up near the top of the list as well. Many teens say they are "going to be rich." In other words, teens have different values than they did a few years earlier.

Despite the unrealistic nature of many of these goals, teens want their hopes and dreams valued. They want encouragement and support, not statements such as "That's ridiculous," or "Don't be silly."

> *"Children don't want a lot of pressure coming from their parents. They don't want to always live up to the parents' expectations. Kids want to set their own goals not to fulfill the parents' goals." – Nancy*

Dale has similar ideas:

> *"Encouragement of a child's dream for a future career is needed because a child will not perform in something he doesn't even like."*

As difficult as it may be, encourage whatever dream or career goal your teenager may have. Encouragement gives them the sense of worth and individuality we have been discussing. Pointing out the impracticality of the goals squelches self-esteem. Going one step further and trying to impose goals parents want for them brings resistance and rebellion.

Sports is an interesting example. Careers in professional sports are lucrative and envied. Many young teens dream of a professional sports career, and parents can't lose by supporting these dreams. If the teen is not good enough, it will become apparent without you shooting down the idea. Unfortunately, it is frequently the parents who want a sports career for their teen, sometimes for selfish reasons (although they don't always realize this). Jason has obviously experienced this:

> *"Parents sometimes push their kids in sports a little too much. It discourages us when the parents want more than we want. Or it might boost their image. If the kids are really going into sports maybe push them a little but*

if they don't like it or are not happy don't push them. It
will make matters worse."

But discuss the relative merits of career goals, even point out some flaws in the plan. Warning: don't try to persuade teens of the folly of their plans or impose your own ideas on them. As teens get older and further into their education, they tend to become more realistic but they still may not be in agreement with parental goals and aspirations. Whether they have realistic goals, or what you see as a dream, discuss, support and encourage. This respect will pay big dividends later as teens will be more prone to come to you for advice when they need it. If you ridicule and/or impose, communication will be shut off. Let's give Amanda the final word on the subject of goals and dreams:

> *"For a career I want to be a ballet dancer. My parents*
> *want me to be a lawyer or doctor. They don't support me*
> *enough and it makes me feel really alone. I don't know*
> *why they can't accept the fact that ballet is one of the*
> *only things that makes me happy and I want to devote*
> *the rest of my life to study and perform it."*

By now Amanda may have already abandoned this dream. While the loss of a dream can be a disappointment, the lack of respect shown by her parents for her hopes was probably even more disappointing.

Respect and Trust

Respect and trust are closely related in the area of decision-making. Respecting a teen's decisions is another way of saying "I trust you." When a teen wants to attend a party where alcohol will be served, this decision is respected by the parents when they allow her to go, and the teen is trusted not to indulge at the party.

Remember Rob's dilemma of having spent $1,000 on baseball cards? The parents respected his decision to look after the money from his paper route himself. They trusted him to spend it wisely. Rob may have blown this trust, as offspring occasionally will, but the respect his parents showed him by not making him turn over his earnings to them was no doubt very much appreciated.

The opportunity to show respect presents itself almost daily. Teens look for their choices to be respected regarding friends, money, clothing, and privacy. (The importance of these areas to teens was discussed in the Introduction.) These aspects of teen life are absolutely vital to them. How do you decide which of the teen's decisions you will respect and which you will overrule? Diana's mother says:

"If it's not life threatening, it's OK."

While this may be an understatement, it's close to what works best with teens. The example of clothing comes to mind. Parents want their teens to look nice. After all, the child's appearance is not only a question of teaching the importance of dressing respectably, it also reflects on the parents. But teens want to fit in with their peers. Looking nice and fitting in sometimes coincide, depending on the fashion of the day. When they conflict it is in no way harmful to respect the teen's decision. There are two deciding factors.

One is, how vital is the issue? As we have seen, friends and fitting in with them is one of the most crucial factors in teenage life. The other factor is respect for the teen's decision. Wearing chartreuse jeans, a purple T-shirt, and a bowler hat may look funny to an adult, but it's not life-threatening and it suits teen taste. One of my students came in to see me about this very point:

> A 15-year-old girl came into my counseling office one day to talk about how strict her parents were. When I asked her for examples, she discussed her curfew, the fact she did not receive an allowance, and her parents' dress code. She had to wear a dress and leather shoes to school every day. None of her friends wore dresses — in fact, none of the girls at the school did. I suggested we meet with her parents to discuss these issues. She agreed; however, there

was no need to discuss clothing as she kept a pair of jeans and some T-shirts in her locker and changed every day anyway.

Despite the severe consequences of disobeying her parents, this girl would rather take her chances of being caught than wear nonconforming clothing. While she had solved this problem, the relationship with her parents was strained because she did not feel that they respected her. The message they were giving was "You are not capable of looking after yourself, so we'll do it for you." This is not a message teens want to hear. They very much want to believe that, in many ways, they can handle themselves.

The same goes for teen decisions about privacy. Jamie has a problem with her parents:

> *"I'm on the phone a lot, I have my own line. They get mad 'cause I'm always in my room."*

How can it hurt anyone if they want to spend hours at a time in their room? They need the space from the family or they wouldn't do it. No threat to life — no problem.

How about the 13-year-old who decides she wants to go to the midnight showing of *The Rocky Horror Picture Show?* Probably not. There are dangers when a young girl is out at night. Saying "no" is well within a parent's rights. It is best, though, to explain the reason calmly. The teen still may rage and storm, but the parents have done their job in the best possible way. Remember, teens are "walking hormones" — they aren't able to be sensible all the time. Parents who care will not accept every decision the teen makes, just the ones where they can't hurt themselves.

The most difficult area in which to respect teen decisions is that of friends. Most parents would love for their teen to be friends with the top student in the class, but it doesn't always work this way. The top student may be interested only in academic activities, not social ones.

The rule to follow is "Friendships can't be legislated."

Does this mean that parents should say nothing about their teen's friends if they disapprove? Not completely, but a better way to handle this situation is to take a look at what needs these undesirable friends are fulfilling for the adolescent, and try to meet the needs in other ways. Seek counseling if the answers are not apparent. Attacking friends directly does not work. Be patient. If the teen has absorbed your family values, he will soon see that the friendship is potentially dangerous and drop it. This is a lot to ask, but the respect shown for these decisions is much appreciated and will pay off in the long run.

RESPECT AND UNDERSTANDING

With the onset of puberty comes a flood of new and puzzling feelings. Teens can't always explain how or why they feel that way, they just do. Understanding these feelings, or at least trying to, is taken by the teen as a sign of respect.

> *"I have a bad day and am grouchy sometimes. My parents blow up at me when I act grouchy towards them." – Jamie*

While this reaction is understandable, it doesn't work. Getting mad at anyone who is in a bad mood is just asking for a fight. In this case a little humor could deflect the anger or frustration. If nothing funny comes quickly to mind, give the teen some space and possibly try to talk to him or her later. Always remember who the parent is.

Does this mean you have to tolerate disrespect and verbal abuse? No way! If your teenager's frustration leads to that, state clearly that such language is unacceptable and suggest strongly that they calm down in their room. Understanding a teen's feelings shows respect for what they are going through, but you do not have to compromise your standards to do so.

Teens show emotion through silence. Asking what the problem is can be met with "I don't want to talk about it." Again, the most effective strategy is to allow some space, and see if they want to discuss it later. Since parents know that many teen problems are relatively trivial, there is a tendency to minimize them with statements like "Don't be silly" or "Quit acting like a baby." This immediately communicates a lack of understanding, by not respecting the significance of the concern. To teens, every issue assumes the proportions of a Middle East conflict.

Finally, respect for feelings can be shown by not making fun. This is particularly true with regard to boy-girl relationships. Teens are raw-nerve sensitive about these relationships, possibly because they aren't sure how to deal with them. Fathers are especially prone to joking about boyfriends or girlfriends. They mean well but teens do not appreciate the lack of understanding. Talk about the relationships, but be careful not to even inadvertently make fun of them.

Since communication, trust and understanding are all involved in respecting teens' ideas, opinions and dreams, "Hear Me" and "Trust Me" are both cornerstones of this process.

SHOWING RESPECT FOR TEENS

- Listen and give consideration to their ideas, opinions and dreams.
- Let them make decisions — as long as the consequences for making the wrong one are not serious.
- Try to understand their feelings.

7

Responsibility — Me?

((They don't give me enough responsibility.
They won't let me grow up. My Mom sometimes
asks me if I need help with my hair or if I
can't decide what to wear, she picks things
out for me. I mean, I'm almost 13 years old.))
– Alison

7. Help develop RESPONSIBILITY

There is no area of parenting in which you will spend more emotional energy than in helping your teen develop a sense of responsibility. While full blown disciplinary situations can be extremely draining emotionally, at least they are relatively infrequent. The teaching of responsibility is almost daily. The constant little battles over chores alone can wear parents down, more than the infrequent blow-ups.

If you have never given it much thought you may be wondering, why bother if the process of developing responsibility is so draining? The type of person you end up with, is the answer. Responsible adults have to be accountable for their actions. If they don't get a presentation done in time, they lose the client. If they don't pay for an expensive purchase, it's repossessed. Teaching responsibility to teens makes them accountable for their actions in the "real" world.

Responsible adults are also self-disciplined. If there is a job that needs doing, they do it without being told. If work isn't done, they take it home. Teaching teens to clean up their living area and to get their homework done on time helps develop self-discipline.

Finally, responsible adults are considerate of others. They respect other people's feelings and sensibilities. They try not to be biased and racist, but instead to consider all people equal. They show up to meetings on time so that others aren't kept waiting, and try not to embarrass others through their actions. Teaching manners and punctuality to teens help them become considerate people.

We all want our teens to develop responsibility, partly because it helps lead to success as an adult. Every parent wants their child to be successful, hopefully even more successful than they are, because success can be the path to happiness.

Another reason for wanting to develop responsibility — a lesser one which still carries weight — is that parents generally feel that their child's behavior reflects how successful they have been as parents. Their image is at stake if their 13-year-old belches loudly in a restaurant. If their teen gets sent home from school for cheating on a test, parents may feel ashamed and embarrassed.

> *Teens want to become responsible as well, because it leads to trust, which in turn leads to more freedom.*

Teens want to become responsible as well, because it leads to trust, which in turn leads to more freedom. Teens don't consciously realize this at first, but they quickly discover that consistently getting their chores done results in being able to stay out later or go out more often.

And being responsible makes a teen feel he or she is a contributing part of the family, more adult. It helps them to believe they are growing up, a feeling that is critical at this age.

Does all this heavy parental philosophy mean that teens actually want to be given responsibilities? If so, this is almost as shocking to parents as teens wanting rules. Well, take it from the teens themselves.

When Sally was asked if her parents give her enough responsibility she replied:

> *"No. I don't know. Lots of times I don't think my parents give me enough credit. They always tell me 'Don't do this or don't do that.' I think they're scared I'll embarrass them even though I'm a good kid."*

When asked what household chores she had, Sally's answer was:

> *"Not much and I think I should have more. I don't mind doing work in the house, and I try to. My Mom works like a slave in the house."*

Tiffany had a similar answer:

> *"I sweep the floor and usually vacuum. I'm not expected to do tons of chores, I just do what I do. I think it's fair, I probably should have more."*

It's not only girls who want responsibilities, so that they can become trustworthy young adults. Listen to Richard's thoughts on whether he is being given enough responsibility:

> *"Not really. My parents think I am pretty lazy, they don't realize how independent I can be...I mow the lawn, take out the garbage, clean the kitchen and set the table. I could vacuum and dust the house. But my parents think I'm too lazy so I don't have to do that."*

Branden not only thinks having responsibilities are fair, he even knows why:

> *"Feeding my pets, babysitting, going places all alone, getting things for my Mom, cleaning up my room, doing the dishes, making my bed and vacuuming. This is fair because I'll turn out good in the future because of this."*

Obviously developing responsibility in a teen should be easy — parents want it and so do teens. Why then is it so emotionally draining? The problem arises due to the fundamental nature of teens. While they are almost unanimously in favor of the concept, the actual execution is jeopardized by teenage "stuff." Their concentration span is one problem. The teen might start a task, be distracted by a good show on television, a comic book, or a fight with a sibling. Priorities are another interference. If a friend calls and wants to go to the mall, even Sally — who wants more chores — would probably drop cleaning her room and go. If the distraction has a higher priority (and almost everything does), teens would rather do that than their assigned chores. They mean well, but they do not yet have the self-discipline to carry out the duties without constant reminders. This should not be unexpected. After all, a reason for assigning responsibilities is to help *develop* self-discipline.

> **A reason for assigning responsibilities is to help develop self-discipline.**

The result of all this is that we have the proverbial road to hell, paved with teenage good intentions. The raw material is there, but parents are the ones who have to shape it. The shaping is where the "emotional sweat" enters the picture. It's hard work but the resulting responsible young adult is well worth the effort. An examination of the major areas involved in developing responsibility will show us where the problems are, and hopefully how to deal with them.

HOUSEHOLD CHORES

Few would argue that one of the best ways to teach responsibility is to ensure that teens have to do household tasks. Problems can arise in two areas:

1. **Balance** — between the number of tasks given and free time, as well as balancing these tasks between siblings.
2. **Enforcement** — getting the teens to finish their chores.

Balancing Chores

HOW MANY IS ENOUGH

Determining a balance between the number of chores a teen has and their free time causes many family arguments, but communication and going in armed with knowledge help keep disagreements to a minimum. As in the setting of rules, sitting down with the teen peri-odically to discuss responsibilities is useful. Again, this could be a yearly event. Knowledge comes through finding out what other parents are doing. You don't have to follow others, but at least you will know what is common practice.

The natural starting place for assigning household chores is the teen's own living space. We have already discussed the norm — teen bedrooms are usually a mess. It is not unreasonable to expect some sort of order, at least a weekly clean-up. Those who have the luxury of their own bathroom, or one shared just with siblings, should probably be responsible for cleaning all or part of this room as well. Even to a teen it makes sense that if they use it, they are responsible for it.

Let's look at some teen comments on what they do around the house and what they think of their responsibilities.

> *"I babysit, empty the dishwasher, set the table. Yes it is fair because both parents work and they need help." – Courtney*

> *"I have to mow the lawn, shovel the walks, clean my room, vacuum. I think this is just fine having these chores because I earn money." – Jon*

> *"• clean washroom*
> *• clean my room*
> *• sweep the floor*
> *For me I don't think this is fair, I always work all the time." – Rosemarie*

"The household chores I have are making my bed, cleaning my room and putting away my coat and shoes when I come in. I think it's fair and I think I should stay with this many." – Ryan

"Cleaning my room, washing dishes, taking out garbage, shovel walks, mow lawn. I think these chores are fair but for my allowance I think I should do fewer." – Andrew

As you can see there is some variation both in jobs and in opinions. The great majority of teens thought that their responsibilities were fair enough. Tara's response added a note of reality:

"I have to vacuum the house and occasionally do the dishes. I guess it's fair, I just hate doing it."

Achieving a balance between free time and chores should not be difficult. Check with other parents, then discuss the topic with your teen. Compromise until both sides agree the load is fair.

BALANCING BETWEEN SIBLINGS

If there was one common complaint among teens about balance, it was that brothers or sisters did not do their fair share. This is indeed a thorny issue. Should younger children do the same amount as older ones? (probably not) and should boys have the same number of jobs as girls? (probably). You need effective communication to distribute the chores as fairly as possible. If you think you will ever completely end the complaints, though, you're dreaming. Personalities and rivalries will always create arguments and bickering.

Let's allow some of our cross-sample of teens to speak on these points.

"I have to clean the bathrooms every week, I also end up doing other chores which are for other people to do. It is not fair. I do my chores and they do not do theirs and I have to do it for them." – Mark

"I like to help out and I will. It's just when my brother the couch potato does nothing it makes me mad because he's still my Mom's favorite." – Sally

"I have to water the plants, do the dishes, vacuum, clean my two rooms, groom the dog. No it's not fair my 10-year-old brother has to take out the garbage. I think I should have fewer." – Shannon

Why don't these teens say something to their parents? The fact is that even in very close families, most teens are either afraid or too shy to raise what they consider to be sensitive issues like rules and chores. Basically, they are afraid that their parents will be upset with them — even when there is little cause for this thought. It takes several years of working on family communications to get them to the point where teens will bring up concerns themselves. If this happens at all, it most often comes in the mid to late teens. Parents, the adults, have to be the ones to be periodically checking on the state of the union by holding family meetings, or listening carefully to mumbled complaints.

"I empty the dishwasher, clean my room. Other miscellaneous things. Sometimes I think I do too much but when I really take in perspective what my parents do, I hardly do anything." – Kelly

Ensuring Chores Get Done

Finally we reach the part most parents have been waiting for. Never mind all that philosophy about why you're giving out chores, how do we get the kid to do them? How indeed? In short, with patience and persistence.

1. Remember, most teens do not live primarily to get their chores done. They have higher priorities. Keeping this thought in mind will help you not take their apparent laziness personally. They are neither lazy nor trying to upset you. They are just disorganized, active, social beings who would rather be with their friends,

watching TV or reading a magazine than working at boring, tedious household chores. Can you really blame them?

2. Do not assume anything. Do not assume they will remember their duties. Do not assume that because you told them to clean up their room, it will be done. Do not assume that because they have started a job they will finish it.

3. Start by setting a schedule. Teens function best when there is a routine. If dishwashing is a duty of each kid, either post a schedule of who works which night, or set up a system; for example Joey has Monday, Wednesday and Friday, while younger brother Billy has Tuesdays and Thursdays. Keep things simple but clear. Some tasks, like cleaning, laundry and vacuuming should be done weekly. This is especially true when it comes to room-cleaning. The rest of the week, just close the door and don't worry about it. Even food doesn't get (very) moldy in a week.

> *Remember, most teens do not live primarily to get their chores done. They have higher priorities.*

4. Weekly jobs should be done on the same day to establish a routine. Saturday mornings (not too early) are an excellent time for chores since parents are usually available to supervise. Once a routine is established, the rule is clear. The teen goes nowhere until the chores are done.

5. Patience and Persistence. If there is no sign that your teen has remembered the task, remind her. You may need two or three reminders. Stay calm but watch to see if she actually starts. Remember, you cannot assume. My son had a clever habit of always agreeing cheerfully, then going back to his book. If we got busy with our own chores and assumed his cheery acknowledgment meant that he was starting this chore, nothing got done. He meant to get at it, but got engrossed in the book and "forgot."

Once the task is started, check frequently but not obviously. If progress stops, remind again. Don't become upset. Maintain a sense of humor — it's not hard when you remind yourself that the reluctant behavior is normal. You might even try to remember way back to how you felt about chores (be honest, though).

POSTING NOTES

One approach worth a try is to post a note somewhere where the errant teen is sure to see it. This can reduce confrontation and snarky answers, but still gets the reminding done.

HUMOR

As much as possible, try to keep the reminders to do chores light. Teens respond to shouting with anger and resentment, which you certainly don't need on a daily basis. Try using some humorous lines instead, no matter how corny.

WHAT WORKS FOR ONE

The mother of two children, one a young teen, the other two years younger, was fascinated with the work ethic of a friend's son. This lad was in his late teens. Each morning when he got up, he immediately made his bed and tidied up his room. Everything in the room was neat, clean and organized. The mother of the two children was impressed and asked the friend how she taught her son to be so neat. The friend replied that years ago she had simply told her son that he could not leave his room each day before he had tidied it up. The habit had been with him ever since.

Naturally, the young children's mother wanted her kids to be this responsible, so she immediately instituted the system in her home. No way. Her children not only did not resent being kept in their rooms, they quite enjoyed it. After the kids were late for school a couple of times, she gave up and went back to a weekly system. What works with one child does not necessarily work for others.

"My parents (mostly my Mom) argue with me about our chores mainly. Either we (my brother and I) don't finish on time (every Thursday) or we didn't do them right."
– Thora

When the chores are finally completed, then the teen can go and do whatever, while you relax for a while. If you are not sure that all the reminding and checking are worth the effort, reread the start of this chapter about the purpose of building responsibility. The reminders, etc., should only continue until the teen gets into a habit. Some will eventually become self-starters, while others will always need reminders. Even with the last type, they won't need as many, or as much checking up. This is especially true when they discover that there is no way in this world that they are going to get out of those chores. Organization, patience and persistence, reminding and checking (not nagging) should ensure the jobs get done. If this still doesn't work, consequences are in order.

ALLOWANCE

"I get enough allowance to get by. I don't get a lot but I've learned the value of money and how to invest and save it." – Paul

Learning to handle money is an important component of responsibility. Everyone has heard horror stories of adults who loaded their charge cards to the limit and eventually had to declare personal bankruptcy. Adults have to be fiscally responsible, so it is best to teach teens these skills early.

Let's start out with a basic principle. All teens need a source of money that they can control, in order to learn how to deal with it responsibly. Giving a teenager money whenever he needs it teaches nothing. In adult life there is no one who is going to give you money any time you require it. Why not start teaching this early?

> **All teens need a source of money that they can control, in order to learn how to deal with it responsibly.**

Sometimes a source of money can be obtained through babysitting, or other such casual jobs, but these are rarely a regular source of income. An allowance that can be counted on to arrive on schedule parallels a salary in the adult world. Just as adults have to try to make this amount last until the next pay day, teens need to stretch their allowance until the next one arrives, or they are broke. Giving an allowance is both realistic and effective financial training.

To productively teach financial responsibility, there are some guidelines to follow, which the teens themselves are quick to point out. These include the concepts of frequency, amount, and whether or not the allowance should be tied to household chores.

Frequency

Since teens do not have much self-control and budgeting ability to begin with, a weekly allowance schedule is the most effective. Jeff, for example, is happy with his allowance except that:

> *"The only bad thing is I get paid at the beginning of the month, and it's gone at the end."*

Many of us have the same problem! Parents who get paid monthly probably find it easier to give out allowance on the same schedule, but this is hard on teens. Once a week is best.

Once the frequency has been established, a specific time will also help. This is as much for parents as it is for the teens. Without a standard day and approximate time, parents tend to forget. As we have already discussed, many teens have difficulty asking for things, and money is one of them. Jon has this problem:

> *"I don't get enough because my parents always find some way to forget about my allowance."*

Ashlie has the same difficulty:

> *"They said they would give me $10 a week, but sometimes I have to remind them."*

Setting a day and approximate time, for example Friday at supper time, gets everyone into a routine, and serves as a reminder.

> *"I argue with my parents mostly about money. I always want more money and my parents already think I get too much. I spend most of my money on clothes, but it goes so fast and then I get angry about how little I can buy with my allowance. My parents always tell me to*

save it, but I'm the type of person that spends it as fast as I can — at least that's what my parents say, but I don't agree. I'll save it for a while, but when I'm saving there are other little 'necessities' I need (such as make-up, magazines, and lunch at Dairy Queen). – Shannon

Shannon is typical of most teens — they're trying to be responsible with money, but don't quite have the hang of it yet.

Amount

There are three effective ways to decide how much allowance to give a child.

1. Take into account the cost of the things that teens need or want to spend money on. This depends on the breakdown of what you expect your teen to buy out of the allowance and how much these things cost. For example, are bus fares and lunches paid for by parents or from the allowance? Does your teen have to pay for clothing? Are special events like movies and the amusement park to come out of the allowance, or do parents cover the cost? Once it has been decided (preferably together) what is to be paid for from the allowance and the cost of these things has been calculated, set a figure. Tara says:

   "I think I get enough allowance because I have enough to buy clothes and stuff. Your parents should give you money according to what you are expected to buy. If you're expected to buy all your clothes with $5 a week, that's not good."

   If you don't want your teens pestering you for money frequently, set the amount high enough so that it includes the things that they frequently have to spend money on. These are recurring expenses such as bus fares and lunches (if you or your teen doesn't make them), and clothing if you are using this type of system.

2. Ask other parents what they give. This should probably not be a method by itself, since it is not tailored to your teen. Using an average of other parents' allowances is fine as long as the expectations of what they are going to do with the money are the same.

"For the allowance I get I think I should have more because of the chores. I think my parents should say how much they are giving you and how much you want and meet in the middle." – Andrew

3. Take into account chores, which is in fact paying the teen for work done. There are conflicting philosophies on this issue. Some parents believe that teens should be responsible enough to help out around the house without being paid for it. They then set allowances without regard for what teens do as chores. Barbara Coloroso, a highly respected parenting expert, agrees with this school of thought. Others feel that since you are paid for your work in the real world, the same applies at home and they therefore tie the allowance amount to how much work gets done. Both of these viewpoints have validity.

Interestingly, most teens seem to believe that allowances should be related to chores. Here are some examples:

"I think my allowance should be more since I do lots and also have to pay for my own clothes. They should decide by how many chores we do and what our needs are." – Tara

"Yes I get enough allowance. My parents decide on how much allowance I get by how much I do around the house." – Kent

"I don't get allowance at all, which for a while I thought was unfair. But then I thought about it and realized that I don't have any real chores. I think you should have to

do chores to get an allowance. So I think my parents should set up a list of weekly chores for each child, and each chore is worth a certain amount. And each time you don't do a certain chore, then some money should be taken off your allowance." – Amy

The one advantage to tying the allowance to chores is that you have an automatic consequence for failure to do them, namely deducting allowance. If you have followed the Patience and Persistence method outlined earlier you will not often need a consequence. Occasionally though, parents get busy themselves and don't have time to supervise. In these cases it would be reasonable to subtract part of the allowance if the chore did not get done. Keep calm though. It should be little more than a statement — you didn't clean your room this week so you lose $2. End of discussion.

Perhaps your system could be a combination of straight allowance and payment for chores — a sort of salary plus commission. The teen would get a base amount, no matter what, plus an equal amount contingent on the completion of his chores. This would ensure that, if the teen had a bad week, he would not be left with no money at all.

No matter what system you use, teens need a steady income in order to learn how to deal with it. Parents could further this financial training by teaching their teens to save a certain percentage of their allowance — a pay-yourself-first system. Even if the allowance does not afford enough leeway to do this, learning to pay expenses out of a fixed amount should be encouraged.

"I get enough to get the things I need and enough to learn the value and responsibilities to having money." – Keith

HOMEWORK

Most parents would agree that a responsible teen is one who does his or her homework regularly. This definitely leads to better grades and what parent doesn't want their teen to do well in school? Getting the teen to do the homework, though, can be a constant source of arguments. Adolescents don't really know much about the best methods for finishing homework. They consider it a chore and would rather not do it.

From a parental standpoint, the most effective approach is to treat homework like any other chore, with the exception of not subtracting allowance for failure to do it. Set a regular time when homework is to be started, along with the same quiet place, preferably the teen's room. Same time, same place every day, in order to establish a habit.

The parents' job is to see that the work gets done — not to do it. Parents should ensure the teen goes to the designated place at the appointed hour. Here, you should assume in order to build trust. You assume the work is being done unless you find out otherwise, through parent-teacher interviews or report cards. If it isn't, closer supervision is necessary. (See Chapter 14 for more details.)

Much of the topic of responsibility falls into the "Trust Me" category. The more responsible teens are, the more they can be trusted and the more trusted they are, the more responsible they will usually be.

DEVELOPING A RESPONSIBLE TEEN

- Assign chores.
- Balance the number of chores and who does them.
- Check that chores are being done. Remind gently but consistently.
- Give a regular allowance.
- Be patient but persistent.

8

Love Me

**((My parents show me that they care by getting
me something. But I don't want that. I want
them to say that they care about me.))**
– Brian

8. Show signs of CARING

In describing the "ideal" parents, the majority of teens polled included
parents showing that they care. Phrases such as "kind and loving,"
"caring and loving," or "show they love their children" appeared over
and over again. Sometimes the teens described ways of showing caring such as "gives hugs and kisses," "comforting" and "parents who
can be there for their children through rough times."

No matter what the words, there is no doubt teens want signs that
their parents love and support them. Their frantic pace of living, their
constant desire to be with friends, and their frequent need for privacy all suggest that teens don't want anything to do with their care-
takers. Nothing could be further from the truth. Family life may not
be a Number One priority anymore, but it is still high on the list.

A feeling of insecurity is part of being a teen. A separate identity
has not yet fully formed and they are only dimly aware of what their
capabilities are, and what assets they have. Teens are like butterflies

142

emerging from their cocoons to test their wings — without letting go of the branch. For teens, parents are the branch, their home base. They flutter their wings by pushing limits, demanding freedom, and loudly asserting their "rights." But they are not yet ready to fly solo. Reassurance that they are loved and valued, that their parents are there for them when things go wrong and they feel like they're going to fall off that branch, are what you can give them.

> *A balance between showing you care and allowing freedom — between protection and overprotectiveness — is the delicate balance you must try to achieve.*

Among the many different ways that parents show they care (and teens are aware of all of them), some are appreciated more than others. A balance between showing you care and allowing freedom — between protection and overprotectiveness — is the delicate balance you must try to achieve.

> *"Unlike many TV shows, my family doesn't show they care about each other by saying 'I love you' or just saying that whatever I did, no matter how bad, was O.K. We show we care about each other by showing a lot of tolerance toward the things we do, or giving me a big punishment for something I did, or by not allowing me to do something that seems harmless, because they have been around and know what can arise from 'harmless fun'." – Curtis*

WHAT TEENS SEEK

Teens are far more observant and sensitive than most parents realize. They know which actions, both obvious and obscure, show parental love. They are constantly seeking these signs of affection, and they will push until they see some. Pushing can take various forms, from simple attention-seeking behavior all the way to breaking rules, just to see what you will do. They want to be reassured frequently that you care.

Hug and Tell

The two most apparent signs of caring that teens notice are *telling them* and *hugging them.*

> *"My parents show that they care about me by saying so. They say that they love me, and they also kiss and hug me before I leave for school in the morning, and when I go to bed." – Callie*

Murray shows the male viewpoint:

> *"My parents tell me they care about me or they hug me. I don't mind either but I appreciate it when they don't hug me in front of my friends."*

Randy notices the difference between how each of his parents show their affection for him:

> *"My Mom says she loves me every night. My Dad takes me places and buys me things."*

For some reason, it is often harder for dads to say these three little words than it is for moms. When Randy speaks of "buying things," he does not necessarily mean big-ticket items like a bicycle or a stereo. Consider how Stephanie knows that her parents care about her:

> *"My parents buy me and my brother chocolate bars every so often for no reason at all."*

Spending Time Together

> *"They should show they care by trying to do things that their children like, with them, instead of doing things*

they like and dragging the kids along, who then unwill-
ingly are forced to enjoy themselves." – Darren

Teens realize that when parents spend time with their kids, they are showing they care.

"My parents care by going to my soccer games and support-
ing me by coming to all my sports and school functions. I
know they care because they give up their time to come to
my activities. They drive me to school every day and push
me to thrive in school." – Christie

Note that Christie realizes that pushing her to do her best in school is a sign of caring. Her parents must be doing just the right amount of pushing or it would be interpreted as nagging. Heather's parents show they care in ways that are obvious to her. Heather appreciates:

"just little things like my Mom will make my favorite
meal, or my Dad will take me out to hit some golf balls
with him."

And Melissa knows her parents care:

"Verbally, my Mom and Dad always tell me they love
me. We spend a lot of time together as a family and I
think that shows how close your family is and how much
your family cares." – Melissa

It is not accidental that these particular teens are not only success-ful students and athletes, but leaders in their classrooms. The obvi-ous signs of caring shown by their parents have given them more than an average amount of self-confidence, so they do not fear failure when they try new activities. Teens with low self-confidence will not try sports or student leadership activities. Some do not even work hard at their studies, in case they gave it their best and still did not do well. That way they can always rely on the excuse that if they had tried, they would have done better.

Worrying and Rules

Rules both protect the teen and help minimize parental worrying. They don't prevent it, though. The fact that teens realize that worry-

> **Teens realize that worrying, setting rules, and giving out punishments are part of the way parents show they care.**

ing, setting rules, and giving out punishments are part of the way parents show they care, is fascinating. They know these things are necessary and consider them attributes of good parents. This knowledge is heartening, because many parents avoid disciplining their teens for fear they will lose their teen's affection. In fact it is just the opposite.

Young teens show much insight on the correlation between discipline and caring. Vikki clearly supports this idea:

"They take me places, hug me, tell me they love me. And when I do something wrong they punish me so I won't do it again and I get mad but I know they are just caring about me and they don't want me to get hurt."

Michelle also thinks along these lines:

"They show they care a lot. They watch out for me, but still let me have my freedom. If they think something I'm about to do will hurt me, they will let me know.

Darren has given this subject some thought:

"My parents don't seem to be the mushy 'I love you' type, but they do care, which I can tell because they always make a big deal about doing things together. And they always seem worried about where I am and when I'll be home. I know they care because of that fact that they are protective."

Being There

Teens appear to need their parents less and less as they strive for independence. Freedom can be frightening at times, however, and the teens realize this. They still need their parents to listen to them and help them with complicated issues. By taking the time to listen and to advise, parents are showing they care.

"They always help me to solve problems. They usually try to talk with me and try to know more about me."
– Jenny

A fine line exists between trying to get your kids to talk to you about a problem, and allowing privacy. In Chapter 2 we discussed the idea that teens may need some time before they are ready to talk. If they don't want to talk about what's troubling them right away, maybe they will be ready at bedtime, or the next day. In Lyndsey's words, parents can help "by giving you space but always being there to help you."

Paul recognizes his parents' ability to help solve teen problems when he says:

> *"Well whenever I'm down about a girl or something they're always there to bring me up. They show affection for me."*

It doesn't take much time to listen, and this is often enough. Sometimes teens simply need to vent their frustrations, fears or anger. If parents lend a ready ear, the teens will pour out their troubles.

And a Few More Ways

Some ways of showing love and affection are not easy to categorize. Teens recognize them anyway.

> *"The way my Dad shows he cares is he likes to joke around with me. The way my Mom shows she loves me is she writes little notes to me thanking me for the work I do for her." – Megan*

> *"My Dad teases and roughhouses with me lots, he also helps me with my homework and other problems. Dad also hugs me a lot. My Mom writes little happy notes and puts them in my lunch, she also sits down with me when the other kids are at school and we talk, go out for lunch, watch soaps (I wasn't allowed until this year), I really love my Mom." – Naomi*

The common factor in how the fathers of Megan and Naomi show affection is their ability to relax and show they enjoy being with them. It may not seem like a big effort, but the teens clearly appreciate it.

A method that works well for many families, but which is not used much because of the time and effort needed, is "family time." This is a specific period of time, say once a week, where the entire family gets together for activities, talks, or both. The idea seems to work in Rochelle's family:

> *"The way my parents show me that they care is by having family time, in this time we do something together and also talk about what has happened in our lives."*

Family time works best if you start well before the children become teens. Once it is an established family tradition, it is easier to maintain. Family time does not have to be elaborate. It can be as simple as watching TV together and eating a pizza every Friday night. Or, family time can mean a more structured setting, in which the family discusses problems that have come up during the week. Even when teens become more socially active, they will still respect this time period if it has already been well-established.

BALANCING CARING

While showing you care is essential, it can be overdone to the point where the adolescent feels smothered. It is important to strike a balance between caring and being overprotective. The issue of trust comes back into the picture here.

> *"They try to protect me from everything, and they are continually nagging at me. I can't stand it, I wish they'd give me some freedom." – Tara*

Tara's solution:

> *"Say 'I love you' and protect me a LITTLE."*

Emily has a similar concern:

> *"I think that they try too hard. They care too much and get into your business."*

Concern with overprotectiveness is uppermost in Derek's mind:

"My Mom is probably the most overprotective mom in the world. The first time she left me home with my 19-year-old friend to watch me and went with my father out for dinner she called six times in one hour to see if I was alright. I don't mind the overprotectiveness but sometimes it bothers me."

Obviously, trust is of tremendous importance to teens. Lyndsey phrases the idea of balance in teen language. She feels parents should show they care:

"by giving you space and not prying but knowing when to step in. They should try and remember to let us experience with our lives."

> **It is important to strike a balance between caring and being overprotective.**

Michelle has a balanced three-point program for parents to show they care:

"Let us have freedom. Tell us they care. Respect our privacy."

Developing an equilibrium between caring and overprotectiveness is a delicate process. It involves frequent communication with the teen to reach as happy a medium as possible. Caring and trust, therefore, are almost as closely related as caring and communication.

"Usually when I argue with my parents, it's because I feel that they care too much about how I feel, that they don't realize that I don't feel the same way about my life as they do. I feel that my parents think that I am just like they were, but I'm not." – Kevin

While the phrase "Hug Me" obviously is crucial to what teens want from their parents, "Hear Me" (as in listening to your teens when they need to talk) is also an important part of showing you care.

SHOWING YOU CARE

- Tell them frequently you love them.
- Hug them.
- Spend time with them.
- Give consequences for wrongdoings.
- Listen to their concerns.
- Don't yell.

9

Honesty:
The Best Policy

((Sometimes they aren't (honest) to protect
my feelings. But I think I have the right
to know the truth, no matter what it is. **))**
– Tara

9. Demonstrate HONESTY

To most adults, basic honesty means not lying, cheating or stealing. To teens, it means telling the truth — about everything. If there are problems in the family, they want to know about them. If there are sensitive issues that need examination, teens want the subject discussed openly and frankly. If parents are wrong, teens want them to admit it.

It's not that parents mean to be dishonest with their teens; they feel that either the teenagers will not be able to understand the problems, or they don't want them to worry about these things. The flaw in the first argument is that teens are quite capable of understanding problems of all types. Certainly some explanation of them will need to be made, but teens' level of comprehension is high enough to grasp most of the intricacies. The argument about worrying falls apart quickly because teenage antennae pick up indicators anyway, and worry even more about what their parents are keeping from them. Teens usually have vivid imaginations, and if they don't know the details, will imagine the worst. Honesty with full explanations is almost always a far better policy.

CAN TEENS TELL?

Many parents withhold the truth or bend it a little for the above reasons, believing their teens don't know the difference. WRONG! Most teens know very quickly when the truth is being withheld or altered, and resent it. Stephanie is a typical example:

> *"Sometimes my parents aren't honest with me and it makes me mad. I am 14 and I deserve to know what is going on in my family. Besides chances are that I will find out sooner or later anyway. Honesty is very important."*

Andrea relates how she knows her parents are lying to her:

> *"I think my parents are not honest at all. They never tell me what they feel like. I think they try to be honest with me but they do not succeed. If I ask them a question, they'll give me an answer, then if my sister asks the same question, she'll get a different answer."*

One of the real dangers of not telling teens the truth is pointed out by Rochelle:

> *"I don't think my parents are always honest with me. The reason why I say this is because when my grandpa got lung cancer, I found out about his lung cancer from eavesdropping on my parents."*

Rochelle doesn't say so, but she was likely "eavesdropping" because she had picked up hints of a problem from her parents' mood and tone of voice. It is virtually impossible to hide serious problems from teens. They are just too perceptive. It is also a dangerous practice, not only because teens worry more if they only know part of the truth, but because it sets a poor example. Curtis clearly says:

"Sometimes I can tell that they are lying. This bothers me because they always want me to tell the truth."

It is extremely difficult to explain to teens that there are good reasons for lying — or at least for not telling them about serious problems. How can you teach them to discriminate between the so-called "white" lies and the bad kind? It is far easier in the long run to just tell the truth.

"Honesty is important but my Dad never tells the truth. My Mom says it is better to be honest than to be a liar which is so true." – Amanda

Teens *can* tell if their parents are lying to them, or hiding something. Tactics that might have worked in the past will no longer be effective. As Shakespeare wrote in *The Merchant of Venice*, "Truth will come to light."

WHY IS HONESTY IMPORTANT?

Everyone knows why honesty is important. In this case, however, we're looking at it from the teens' side. Why do *they* think honesty in parents is important?

The reason teens give most often is so that they can trust their parents. This may seem backwards, but teenagers want to know that their parents can be trusted too. For one thing, it makes parents easier to talk to, to confide in. For another, it makes the teens feel more secure in their relationship.

> *"I like knowing what is going on. Even if it isn't good it makes me feel a bit more secure, I feel I can trust my parents more than my other friends, because mine are honest with me." – Naomi*

Michelle agrees:

> *"I think my parents are very honest with me. I think that's important because I'm old enough to know what's happening. If there is something wrong, I want to know. I think it also builds more trust in the relationship."*

> *"I think honesty is important because if my parents aren't honest with me, or with each other, then we will not trust each other anymore." – Winnie*

A second reason teens want honesty from their parents is so that they can understand their decisions. This type of honesty is not so much concerned with avoidance or partial truths, but with explanations. The last thing teens want to hear is "Because I said so." Rather, their maturing intellects need to know the "why" of the decision.

"I think it is very important to always be honest. If they want you to do something then they should tell ya why. It's time they realize that we are old enough to understand." – Lyndsey

Sam has a similar concern:

"Honesty is very important for a parent because a parent must get his/her point out clearly. In order to do that they must speak straight out and be very honest."

Brian has this comment on whether or not his parents are honest with him:

"No because when I ask 'Why can't I' my Mom and Dad always make something up or say 'I don't need to tell you the answer'."

What teens interpreted as a lack of honesty is really an inability or unwillingness on the part of parents to explain themselves. When parents resort to hiding behind their parenthood, they may not know why they have made a certain decision—it just feels right. Even stating that you *don't* know why is preferable to teens, because they recognize its honesty. They reject lies or power statements such as "Because we're your parents."

A third reason why teens believe honesty is important is because it sets a good example for them. If parents want honesty in their children (and what parents don't?) then they have to set the example. Cassandra supports this idea when she writes:

"My parents are honest with me because if they weren't I'd be able to tell right away. I think the reason why they're honest with me is because they want me to be honest with them."

Melissa goes so far as to state that honesty is fundamental to family relationships:

"My parents are very honest. Honesty is the key to good parent-kid relationships. If they want us to be honest to them, they have to be honest to us."

Teens know honesty is important and they know why. If you are not honest with them, they can tell. It would seem, therefore, that honesty with teens is indeed the best policy.

How Do You Know How Much To Tell?

"I think that parents sometimes don't tell the truth just to protect us. Like when my grandma was dying of cancer, they just said she was 'sick'. But I knew because my Dad would always come home crying. I don't mind sometimes when they 'shorten' the truth, but they have to know when to tell us." – Marie

This knowing when to tell everything is a tough call. The deciding factor is probably the maturity level shown by the teen. Those who are generally trustworthy and have a close relationship with their parents should be asked if they want to know what is happening. Marie certainly wanted to know about her grandmother, but would she also be interested in the family financial problems? The only way to find out for sure is to ask. Even if they express an interest, they may tune out shortly after you begin. This means that the problem isn't as interesting as they thought. At least you tried to communicate and to be honest.

The opposite side of the picture is expressed by James:

"I think my parents are too honest with me because every time that there's a problem in the house I know about it and I don't really want to know."

If parents are going to err, it should probably be on the side of openness and honesty. The teens can always either tune out or tell you that they are not interested. The great majority of teens spoke in favor of the honest approach. They appreciate the frankness, and the relationship will be closer because of it.

Honesty in terms of family problems is one aspect of the issue. Others, such as openness when discussing sex and personal problems and admitting you were wrong, were covered in Chapter 2. If these areas are still a problem for you, don't worry. Keep trying. The teens want to talk about their personal problems, and parents can be most effective by listening. Ask a few questions, *listen a lot,* offer a little advice. You can't miss if you keep at it.

> *"Honesty is important to me so I know what's going on and how real life will be." – Mitch*

Honesty, then, is an important ingredient in developing close parent-teen relationships. It is a key component of the "Trust Me" part of the "Hear Me, Hug Me, Trust Me" formula.

BEING STRAIGHT WITH YOUR TEEN

- Being honest breeds trust.
- Be open about family matters — ask if they want to know.
- Don't bend the truth — teens can tell.

10

Humor Is Nothing To Laugh At

**❝ I think a sense of humor is important
in a parent to make a tough or
embarrassing moment go by easier. ❞**
– Julianne

10. Display a sense of HUMOR

Teens are virtually unanimous in believing that a good sense of humor in parents is an "ideal" quality. Teens aren't clear on what makes up a sense of humor, and when it should be used. They don't expect stand-up comedy. They don't expect parents to be hilarious, just to lighten up in certain situations.

Everyone has a sense of humor, but to varying degrees. If you happen to be a great storyteller, by all means tell jokes at the supper table or on the way to the mall. If you can't remember a joke ten minutes after it has been told, don't worry. All that teens appear to want is their parents not to be serious *all* the time. Teens need to be able to relax at home, and one of the ways they can do this is when their parents help them see the funny side of things. School and a social life can be serious enough without the addition of a somber home life.

But when do you use humor and when do you listen? It's not that difficult. Take your cue from them to help you decide whether to diffuse the seriousness of a situation with a joke or whether to listen carefully and offer advice.

Using the survey responses as our cue, let's briefly examine the use of humor in parenting your teen.

WHEN HUMOR HELPS

Being able to see the funny side of life is invaluable. The ability to see humor in otherwise serious situations helps everyone to relax and forget the stresses of the day. Georgia's parents apparently can do this:

"I think my parents do have a good sense of humor. They are always making jokes about the politics and newspaper."

On the other hand, when Chris was asked if his parents had a sense of humor he said:

> *"No, whenever I do something or say something I think is funny they always send me to my room, or at a movie when there is a funny part and everybody laughs they don't get it and look confused."*

Sometimes, as Kristin knows, it is very hard to see the humorous side of life:

> *"My Mom has a lot of stress being a single parent. But I try and make her laugh."*

Laughter and relaxation are intimately connected, in that you have to be relaxed in order to make jokes.

> *"My parents always find something funny in any situation." – Julianne*

We know that Julianne enjoys being at home, and can relax there. Humor is a way to set the tone within the home. It's a way to help make home a place to relax and forget about worries, at least for a while.

Humor is also a great pain reliever, both physically and mentally. Hopefully there won't be many opportunities to use humor in physical situations, but if your teen is involved in sports, it may happen occasionally. If the injury is not too serious, a little joking may help to take away some of the hurt.

A more important use of humor is to relieve emotional wounds. Comments on the importance of wit and joking tended to center on parents' ability to cheer teens up. Donna, for example says:

> *"Yes, a sense of humor is important. When I am feeling sad, my Dad tells me a joke to get me out of a bad mood."*

Janelle has similar thoughts and thinks humor is important:

"in times of depressing moments and when the child is sad or needs to smile."

Good-natured poking fun at one another helped cheer up Amanda, who relates:

"One day my Mom was making faces at me so I called her a dog and she called me a monkey and then we called each other names all night."

WHEN NOT TO BE FUNNY

Most of the time, a sense of humor is an asset in parent/teen relationships. Occasionally, however, being funny is not appreciated. These are times when teens are trying to discuss a serious issue, when friends are present, or when humor is used to embarrass them.

When teens try to talk about something of serious concern to them, they don't like to be made fun of. It is one thing to try to lighten them up when they've done badly on a test, or lost a big game. It's another to make fun of them when they are expressing an opinion, or if they need to talk to you about a serious concern.

"I think a sense of humor is important in a parent so when you're feeling down they can cheer you up. Only in minor cases because if you're feeling down a lot and your parents try to cheer you up, you might take it the wrong way." – Erin

The question becomes, how can you tell if joking will work or not? There is probably no way to be absolutely certain, unless you are unusually perceptive. The best rule is: "If in doubt, try humor first." If the teen reacts with anger or frustration, switch to "listening mode."

Teens also seem to want their parents to appear "parental" in front of their friends. They don't appreciate the teasing and joking that goes on in a family happening in front of peers. When asked if a sense of humor is important, Andrea agrees conditionally:

"Yes! But when the time and place is right. (No personal family jokes in front of friends.)"

Tracy gives an example:

"I was sitting in the car with my Dad when my ex-boyfriend walked by, he goes 'Hey, it's Tracy!' and my Dad yells 'No it's not!' (hah! hah! hah!). That was so humiliating!!"

On paper this incident may seem pretty trivial, but the attempt at a joke in front of a peer was embarrassing for this teen.

Despite these apparent limitations, it is better to have joked and lost than never to have joked at all. If you try a joke and fail, back up and take a different approach. You haven't really lost anything.

Humor loosely falls into the "Hear Me" category, in that you have to be "hearing" what your teens are saying about their moods in order to know whether or not humor is appropriate.

LINES FOR ALL OCCASIONS

If you aren't sure what all this talk of a sense of humor is about, the following jokes are typical of the parental variety. The lines aren't that great, but they do the job of relaxing a potentially difficult situation. You can probably come up with much better ones. If not, feel free to use these.

- Are you going to cut the lawn, or should I just buy a flock of sheep?
- The piano is getting lonely. How about giving it some company for an hour or so?
- Are dishes easier to wash when the food dries on them?
- The flies in the kitchen just carried off your sister. Maybe you should take the garbage out.
- I like what you've done with this room, but shouldn't you make a path to the bed?
- We can call off the search and rescue unit now, he's home.
- Your face is droopier than a basset hound's. What's the matter?
- I'm expecting a call from Elvis Presley any time now. Could you get off the line for a while?

Okay, these are pretty bad, but you get the idea. With a little adjustment for individual humor and different situations, this approach can work much better than a heavy-handed style. The teens may complain about how corny you are, but they'll do it with the hint of a smile on their lips.

11

Be With Me

((My parents don't spend enough time with
me but I'm not saying that my parents don't give
me stuff. They give me money but I
wish we would go somewhere together. *))*
– *Shannon*

11. Spend more TIME TOGETHER

All teenagers like to spend time with their parents (unless there were serious family problems during the pre-teen years). This is especially true for the younger teens. As they grow older, and develop separate interests and their own social lives, the amount of time they need becomes less *but it never ends completely.*

Spending time with your teen, however, is not as simple as it sounds. As we have already recognized, each teen is different. Differences mean that parents must try to understand how much time their teen needs with them, and how that time should be spent. This is often a tightwire balancing act, especially if there are several children in the family.

Being with your teenager is even more difficult due to the demands of society. With both parents working in many two-parent families, and with single parents being the family's sole support, parents are often too tired to spend much time with their kids. Weekends are spent catching up on housework and chores.

Fortunately, as we have seen throughout this book, teens can be very understanding. They recognize when their parents are at least attempting to meet their needs, and appreciate these attempts. They also recognize the barriers their parents face in trying to spend time with their kids. Let's look first at these barriers, then at how to overcome them.

THE MODERN CHALLENGE

These are different times than the ones most parents grew up in. Changes in people's attitudes with regard to women in the work force, expectations for a high standard of living, and the breakdown of the institution of marriage have created a far more complex world. Besides parents having to work in order to achieve a privileged lifestyle

(expected, by the way, by teens) there are also more divorces, resulting in more single-parent families. The complexities of modern life create seemingly impenetrable barriers to a rich family life.

While teens recognize these obstacles, they still feel cheated. Courtney's case is typical:

> *"They don't spend much time with me. Both of them work and don't get home till 6:00 p.m. Then I do my homework and they do theirs. On the weekend both of my parents are busy. I would love to spend more time with them."*

Jordan has a similar problem:

> *"They spend an average amount of time with me but I don't think it's enough. I'd like to play hockey, baseball and even go golfing, but my Dad and Mom are always working so they don't have enough time to spend with me."*

The stresses and long hours of many jobs is a major cause of parents' inability to give time to their teens. When they do get home they are tired and often tense. Knowing this, however, does not make the situation any easier to take. Matthew's frustration is evident:

> *"My Dad works all day and when he comes home he's too tired to spend time with me. My Mom works at home. All we hear from my Mom is 'be quiet'."*

Fathers are especially prone to working long hours. It is interesting to note that teens of both sexes miss this contact, even when mother is at home. Stefanie makes this point very clear:

> *"My Dad doesn't (spend enough time with me) because he's in real estate, so he's away a lot. I say this because he comes home late at night. He doesn't take me to sports places and sometimes it makes me mad. My Mom at least talks and asks about school when she comes home. She takes me places (shopping)."*

Karen's frustration shows as she describes her father's daily routine:

> *"I think my Mom spends a lot of time with me. We do lots of things together. My Dad spends some, not as much as my Mom. He has the same daily schedule, wake up, go to work, come home, eat supper, take a shower, watch TV, go to bed. That's what he does every day."*

Chris's need to spend some time with his father is painfully obvious:

> *"I do not think my parents spend enough time with me because my Dad is always at work and my Mom is too boring. So I wish my Dad would take time off work and him and I go fishing or something."*

The other major barrier to giving time to teens is divorce. The need for attention from both parents was discussed above. When there is just one, it is twice as hard to give teens the time and attention they require. Robert reinforces this point by writing:

> *"My parents do not spend enough time with me because my Dad lives in another city and my Mom is always at work."*

Allison feels that her mother does not spend enough time with her because:

> *"She's always with her boyfriend or at work. When she's home, instead of sitting down and watching TV, I'd like to play catch."*

Conflicting schedules also plays a part in keeping parents and kids apart.

> *"My Mom is divorced so she works most of the time and when she comes home I'm usually out with my friends or doing homework." – Patrick*

This is not a putdown of single parents. The responsibilities of earning a living, keeping house and looking after a family place a huge burden on single parents. Even when teens understand this, they continue to resent the lack of time spent with them. Communication, setting priorities and sharing household chores, will all help to overcome this barrier, so that the kids get to spend the time they need with their parent (or parents).

THE SOLUTION

Since teens obviously want and need to spend time with their parents, *some time must be set aside for them.* It doesn't have to be a huge amount, but every family should make it a priority to set aside some time specifically for their kids. This might mean that the housework doesn't all get done — but so what! It will wait, for the kids' needs are NOW. Before you know it they'll be grown up and gone — and you'll be left in a clean house all alone.

> *Before you know it they'll be grown up and gone — and you'll be left in a clean house all alone.*

Spending the Time

> *"I think they should spend more time with me. I want to do things but I feel I'm always second on the list. The only time they spend with me is when I'm in trouble." – Andrew*

In the Introduction I stated that **there is no such thing as "quality time."** Many parents try to convince themselves that occasional major outings, such as a baseball game, are of such quality that they make up for weeks of neglect. While these events do mean a lot to teens, most prefer smaller amounts of your time, more frequently. The events do not have to be special or planned events. Making time for your teen can and should often be spontaneous, such as when your teen makes a specific request or when you notice that the teen needs to be with you. Megan wants her parents to spend time with her:

> *"When I need help, or when I'm lonely, or just when I need someone to talk to."*

Jeremy is of a similar mind:

> *"They should spend more time with us when we're moping around the house. I wish they would at least ask me what's wrong. I wish my Mom would spend time with me when I'm sad."*

The idea of spending time spontaneously is also foremost in Jermayne's thoughts:

> *"They should spend time whenever possible and sometimes no matter what, they should put aside whatever they're doing and play catch, go to the mall, or whatever you like to do with them."*

In other words, sometimes it is a good idea to drop everything. Even fatigue will usually disappear when you start having fun with your kids. Board and card games, video games, walks, bike rides or even routine shopping trips are all effective ways of being together without the need for complex arrangements.

> *"They should spend time with me when they have nothing to do, but sometimes parents tend to do something else when they have time. Maybe when they need to buy something they could take us to the mall with them. Or maybe have family day and go for a picnic. That would be great."* – Kimberley

Spectating

Most teens these days take part in some type of activity. Many play sports, others take dance or music lessons. If they are involved in one of these endeavors, they love it when their parents make time in their busy schedules to come and watch.

Horseback riding is a big part of Robyn's life, and she would like her parents to share it with her. She writes:

> *"We hardly do anything together. The only things we do is eat together, talk, do homework and go out for dinner once a month or two. Whenever I go horseback riding I want them to come along but they don't. My parents hardly go out the door."*

In other words, Robyn's parents do some things with her, but not what she really wants. Sounds like a communication breakdown. Your presence at these events is appreciated because it shows interest and caring. It takes no special arrangement, just time.

Planned Events

Small, daily amounts of time shared are one of the keys to building a strong relationship with your teen, but the planned events are what create good memories. Adil for example writes:

> *"I think my parents should spend more time with me over the weekends. I would like to go more places with them like the zoo, swimming, etc."*

The importance of "dad" in these planned events comes through again and again, with teens of both sexes. This may be because he usually is the busiest, and often the hardest to get close to. Catherine's list of preferred activities includes:

> *"Go skiing, traveling. Going for walks. Biking with my Dad."*

> *"I like it when my Dad and I go to baseball games. I hate going to visit relatives." – Curtis*

These statements are probably made together because when visiting relatives, Curtis can't spend time just with his dad, but must share it with his relations. Moms are typically the better communicators and caregivers in the family, but dad is equally important to teens when it comes to spending time together.

Planned events don't have to be often, once or twice a month is enough for most teens. The list of events preferred by them includes:

- movies
- out for dinner (even fast food counts)
- hockey, football, basketball, baseball games (both sexes)
- picnics
- hiking
- golfing
- drives
- major shopping trips

Family vacations are also excellent for spending time together until the mid-teens, when summer jobs and social life become more important.

Family Night

One technique for spending time with teens is to designate one night a week as "Family Night." Friday is often a good choice, but any convenient night will work. Activities can vary each week, with your teen deciding what to do, or a routine may develop with a favorite food (pizza, hamburgers, etc.) and a rented movie or other special activity. Once the family gets in the habit, nothing should be allowed to interfere. In fact, the kids themselves will insist upon this.

> *One technique for spending time with teens is to designate one night a week as "Family Night."*

Like family vacations, the system will start to break down as the teen becomes more socially active, but it should be maintained as long as possible, as it is excellent for family communication and togetherness.

"My parents should spend time with me during meals and before bed. I like to rent or go to movies with my parents." – Lisa

THE BALANCING ACT

So how do you achieve a balance between spending time and giving space?

> *"I like my parents to take me places, but don't want them to spend every waking hour with me. I would appreciate it if my parents gave me some independence."*
> *– Mitesh*

Rochelle has the same message:

> *"Sometimes I think my parents spend a little too much time with me. I like having my space and I don't like my parents knowing everything about me."*

These teens are not saying their parents should stay away from them, just that they need some privacy and independence at times. Divorce requires you to maintain an even more difficult balancing act.

> *"I feel my parents don't spend enough time with me because my parents are divorced and I only see my Mom on the weekends. In the summer I only see my Dad on the weekends. I don't like being smothered with attention either." – Amy*

The solution to this dilemma is **communication**. Parents should provide the opportunity to spend time together, and ask if the teen wants to participate. If the answer is "no," then simply accept it. As the teen becomes older, the answer will be "no" more frequently. There is no need to take this personally, it just means the need for independence and a life of their own is kicking in. With some teens it starts earlier than others. When asked when he would like his parents to spend time with him, Kent replied:

> *"When YOU want to spend time with them. I would like to go shopping or just some place fun."*

In other words, he enjoys spending time with his parents, but only when he wants and needs it. While this may seem selfish, it is the nature of the beast. The wise parent respects variations in moods, allows space when the teen wants it, and spends time with their teen when the opportunity arises. When you realize your teenager is needing more freedom, it is a good idea to give more lead time in planned family outings — just in case the teen has made plans of his or her own for that period.

At this point in the book you're probably already ahead of me in knowing that spending time with your teens falls into the "Hug Me" section because it shows you care about them. But there is also an element of "Hear Me" in finding the right balance.

All teens like to spend time with their parents, but the amounts will vary. Listening to them will provide the key in determining the most appropriate occasions in which to share this togetherness.

HOW TO SPEND TIME WITH YOUR TEEN

1. Be sensitive to their *moods*. When they're down, they need a parent who's sympathetic. When they're up they need one to do things with.
2. *Respond to their requests.* If they ask to do something with you, do it.
3. *Attend their activities.* Go to their recitals, sports events, plays, etc.
4. *Have a "family night."* Set aside one night a week.
5. *Ask them to do things together with you.* If they don't want to, don't insist, give them their space.

12

Setting an Example

> **❝ I don't think they set a very good example for me because they're always doing the same things they tell me not to do. ❞**
> – *Sarah*

12. Set the EXAMPLE

Because they love their parents, young children want to look up to them, to believe that they are perfect. The only difference with teens is that they are a little more realistic. They accept that people aren't perfect, but they still want to be able to admire their own parents. As a result, teens get very upset when they see their parents doing anything they believe to be wrong or bad — in other words, when parents do not set a good example.

When adults consider the concept of "setting a good example," they are usually thinking of complicated moral and philosophical issues, what is right and what is wrong. Teens are much more specific. They break the subject down into four distinct behaviors: fighting, vices such as smoking and drinking, yelling and losing control, and swearing. Adolescents, naturally, want parents who stay calm and who don't have any harmful habits. These are reasonable requests, but because parents are human, they can be hard to live up to.

FIGHTING

When siblings fight with each other, parents react quickly to end it, usually adding a lecture on getting along with each other. When parents argue with each other, it not only sends a conflicting message (and sets a bad example), it scares the kids. Teens tend to think the worst when they hear their parents fighting, especially with divorce being so common these days. Sharon is obviously concerned about her parents:

> *"I think my parents could improve by not fighting so much. They usually fight at night when they think no one is listening. But I'm usually up listening to every word until one of them storms out."*

When asked if his parents set a good example, David replied:

> *"Yes, but they might try to stop fighting sometimes."*

Clayton wasn't quite so charitable with his response to this question:

> *"NOOOO! They should not fight in front of me (no yelling, no drinking)."*

Julianne writes about a classic example of parents trying to do the right thing but giving the wrong message:

> *"Yes, my parents set a good example for me. My parents could improve by not fighting over how we spend time together as a family."*

Arguments occur in most marriages, which does not necessarily mean that the marriage is breaking down. Nevertheless, teens hate to hear these fights, and they certainly don't set a good example of conflict resolution. The message is simple: when the kids are within earshot, either postpone the battle or find a better way to solve the problem.

THE VICES

Teens hate to see their parents doing things that are harmful to themselves. They want them to live forever. Thanks to public education programs, it is common knowledge that smoking and drinking are unhealthy, so naturally teens would not want their parents indulging in these behaviors.

> *"I don't think my parents set a good example for my brother and I. I say this because my Dad smoked when we were younger, and now my brother smokes."*

> *"They set a good example most of the time but not always. My Dad smokes. That's bad but he tells me that if I ever smoked he would kill me." – Courtney*

The old saying "Do as I say, not as I do" was never very effective. Parents naturally do not want their teens developing harmful habits, even if the parents can't break the same habits. Unfortunately, when kids see the people they love and respect most in the world doing something, the example speaks far louder than the words.

We all have our bad habits, but when these habits are potentially physically and emotionally harmful, teens get worried. While smoking is unhealthy in the long run, drinking can often be immediately bad because it changes behavior. There is so much publicity about this that it is only reasonable for teens to be concerned. Robbie is one of these concerned adolescents:

> *"Sometimes my Dad goes out drinking, and that isn't a good example for a 13-year-old."*

Christina is another:

> *"My Mom sets a good example for me, but my Dad doesn't. A way my Dad could improve would be to not drink."*

YELLING

Here we go again. The subject of yelling keeps coming up. When teens are being disciplined they just hate yelling because they feel it shows their parents don't care about them, and overall, they think it's a lousy way to try to communicate. They also feel it sets a bad example.

> *"Ya, most of the time they do set a good example. But my Dad could improve. He criticizes and yells too much. He is so narrow-minded and he should lighten up a bit."*
> *– Jan*

Donna obviously has a very good relationship with her parents, but she has a similar concern:

"Yes, my parents set a good example for me because they are so loving and caring. The only way they could improve is to stop yelling as much when they get mad."

Closely related to yelling is the loss of one's temper. Again, teens see it as setting a bad example.

"My parents set a good example for me. They don't smoke or anything like that. My mom could improve by not getting mad at me over every little thing. I'm a kid, what's more I'm a teenager! She should be a little more understanding." – Cassandra

Rebecca has similar comments on the example her parents set:

"They lose their temper easily. And when they're in a bad mood, they blame everything on us."

Parents' ability to stay calm and cool is incredibly important to teens.

SWEARING

Despite the fact that swear words are all around us — in the movies, in popular songs and even on television now, teens hate to hear their parents using them. In wanting to look up to them, they see their parents as special people. Even if they use swear words themselves, teens don't like to hear them from mom and dad. Alison is very concerned about this issue:

"My parents swear a lot! They could improve by not swearing so much. At least not around me."

Paul is more specific about the circumstances:

"They could improve by not swearing when they're driving."

Most urbanites can probably relate to that! But teens cringe inwardly whenever they hear expletives from their elders. Swearing is closely related to control of temper, of course, but it was mentioned as a separate issue so often, it deserved its own mention.

REALITY CHECK TIME

If this chapter didn't give you a guilty conscience, you're not human. In real life no one can be perfect. The aim of this chapter is to let you know what bothers the kids, so that you can at least try to control the behaviors that set a poor example. As we will discuss in more detail in the next chapter, occasional lapses in your parenting are expected and understood. The understanding only starts to wear thin when those lapses are constant.

SHOWING YOUR BEST SIDE

- Control your emotions — especially in front of the teens.
- Be a role model.
- Avoid the "Do as I say, not as I do" example.

13

Hear Me, Hug Me, Trust Me

While it is interesting and convenient from a writer's point of view to break parenting teens down into 12 distinct characteristics, it can be confusing for a parent. The list of "do's" and "don'ts" gets so long that it becomes impossible to remember everything. So before you are tempted to throw this book across the room and give up, I will quickly add that the twelve characteristics can be boiled down into one expression: "Hear me, hug me, trust me — and don't yell at me."

You can be a great parent by just remembering and following the ideas contained in that expression.

The 12 points are really an expansion of these basics, and are useful for those who want to make an in-depth study of parenting. The "big three plus one" will help you develop a wonderful relationship with your teens, and will result in great kids. A brief review of these basics will show you what I mean.

HEAR ME

In short, listen to your teen. They want to tell you everything, but as soon as they are put down or sense you're not interested, teens shut up. Listening takes concentration and genuine interest.

Listening, as we have discussed, is the more important part of *communicating* with teens. It is also directly involved in at least five more of the characteristics of "ideal" parents. You cannot really understand much about the modern teen unless you are willing to listen to them to discover their likes and dislikes and their concerns. To be fair, it is vital to listen to the reasons for teen mistakes and misbehaviors. This fairness, as we have seen, is intimately connected to the discipline process as it is important to hear the teen's side of the story, and to listen to their ideas of appropriate consequences, before making judgments as to their innocence or guilt and subsequent sentence. Parents not only show they care about their adolescent children by listening to them, they show respect for them as well. Their adventures, their ideas and even their excuses are well worth listening to for these very reasons. The concept of "Hear Me," therefore, takes in a number of the characteristics that teens want to see in their parents.

A key point to remember about listening is that teens very often do not even want a response. They just want to know that someone cares enough about them to listen. Don't be discouraged when they don't appear to be listening to your advice. They often aren't. They just needed a listener.

Here is a short list of how to listen to your teenagers:

1. *Provide opportunities for them to talk.* The dinner table, the car, or in their room at night are all possible places for discussions.
2. *Prompt them with questions to start the conversation.* You need to be aware of their activities in order to ask the right questions.
3. *Look at them when they're talking.*
4. *Don't interrupt or make judgments unless absolutely necessary.*

5. *Stay calm.* No matter how shocking the subject matter, don't react. Keep your emotions under control.

"An ideal parent for me would be someone who listens. They just listen to my problems and then maybe suggest a solution. My parents are the best. I wouldn't exchange them for the world. They are kind, caring and loving. The thing I like most about my Mom and Dad is that they spend time with us and take us places. In fact, just today my Dad took work off to come to my brother's sports day." – Heather

HUG ME

All "hug me" means is that teens need obvious signs that you care. Hugs are the best, especially when least expected. Almost as good is giving them your time by attending their events, playing card and board games with them, and participating in physical activities with them. As they get older, they may want to spend more time with their friends, but there is always some time for mom and dad.

TRUST ME

Trusting is a more complicated matter than listening or showing you care because it involves taking some risks. It also involves teaching the basics of appropriate behavior through a system of discipline.

Trusting starts by setting rules that are fair for everyone and giving clear reasons for them. This ensures that teens know what is expected of them and why. Being home on time, for example, prevents worrying. Not drinking prevents foolish and often dangerous behavior. Consequences are necessary when rules get broken, so that the teens understand the importance of the rules. Both rules and consequences should be determined as a family, not imposed arbitrarily by parents. This involves good communication.

Once the discipline system is in place, the parent must trust the teen to follow the rules. The rule is "Trust first, give consequences later." In other words, the parent starts by assuming the teen can be trusted. It's part of allowing teens the freedom they crave. Checking up should be a last resort when the teen clearly shows, by repeatedly violating the rules, that he or she cannot be trusted. Tell them you trust them, then follow this statement with trusting actions.

Another aspect of trust is *forgiveness*. Teens will make mistakes. This should result in consequences where appropriate, but should not be followed by a loss of trust or respect. Hand out consequences and forget whenever possible.

Trust is also built up by assigning responsibilities to teens, and trusting them to carry them out. This process takes time, since teens often prefer staring at the ceiling to doing their chores. Given time and patient persistence, trust will gradually be built up.

Trusting also shows *respect* for teens' ability to show good judgment, and to do what they know is right. A few missteps along the way should not be allowed to destroy the trust that has been built up. The mistakes should be dealt with swiftly and effectively, then forgotten.

Yes, it is risky. This world has many dangers, and sitting home waiting for your teen to return from a party or a date is hard. The results of trusting your teen are worth it, though.

AND DON'T YELL AT ME

The importance of staying calm has come up over and over again. Communicating, disciplining, being fair, and caring all involve the ability to *stay calm* and *not yell*. If the parents can't keep their cool, you can bet the teens won't. It is the old question of "Who's in control?" Since the teens are little more than walking hormones, they react to most situations emotionally. Sympathize with their state of being. It is up to the parent to keep the situation under control by keeping everyone calm and cool.

WHAT IF YOU'RE NOT PERFECT?

Kids start out loving their parents. It is extremely difficult to lose this love and affection. Parents who care about their kids can make a lot of mistakes, and still have a great relationship with their teens. This book is designed to make life easier for you, not to make you perfect. There is no need to feel guilty because you did not handle a situation flawlessly. You, too, are a human being and are not expected to be perfect. Just learn from the mistake and carry on. If you care about your teen, you already have the main ingredient for a loving relationship, one which will survive your mistakes.

"My parents are great. They're understanding and I can open up to them and tell them how I feel or what I have done. They are willing to hear my point of view before they open their mouths. My parents give me no curfew, they only have to know where I am and what I am doing. I think they're perfect and I hope to be parents just like them when I'm older." – Sarah

14

When Things Go Wrong

Even in the best of relationships, there are times when things go wrong.

The worst thing a parent can do is to try to assess blame. This won't help solve anything. When a pattern of misbehavior, a persistent problem or a sudden crisis is identified, DON'T PANIC! Hasty and emotional reactions almost never work. A better approach is to sit down with your spouse, a knowledgeable friend, a counselor, or a book like this one and work through the problem.

WHY DO THINGS GO WRONG?

The number one factor leading to difficulties with teens is their own insecurity. Until the onset of puberty, teens are extensions of their parents. Young children mimic their parents' actions, wear the clothes laid out for them, eat the lunches their parents make for them. As teenagers, they try to establish a separate identity by wearing clothing they pick out, demanding independence, listening to music parents don't approve of, and throwing out the lunches (carefully made for them by parents) in favor of chips and soda pop.

Because they are in the process of becoming a separate person, they are unsure of who they are and what they are capable of accomplishing. This is the root of teen insecurity. It makes them quarrelsome, moody and, because they cling to their friends for support, subject to peer pressure.

If this basic insecurity is compounded by other factors, the potential for difficulties increases dramatically. The major compounding factors are:

a. *Genetics*. If you have more than one child, you may already have discovered that some children seem more insecure than others from birth. While one child may play by herself for hours on end, the other clings to his parents for support. Where one confidently tries new activities, the other sticks to the tried and true. It is the last group who may be in danger during adolescence. They will be more prone to peer pressures like smoking, sex and alcohol than will their more secure siblings. This doesn't mean all insecure children will experience more teen problems; but the possibility exists. Maintaining communication with these teens is vital to preventing future problems from developing.

b. *Dysfunctional Families*. This is the one everyone knows about. In fact, when teens get into trouble these days, most people tend to blame the family. But this is not always the cause. Still, there is no question that many problems with teens are the result of families that don't function well. Dysfunctional families may have an alcoholic or abusive parent or parents, parents who argue constantly, or even parents who are not home often due to their jobs. They can also include parents who do not spend enough time with their teens even when they are home, and parents who are wrapped up in their own pursuits. All these circumstances can increase a teen's insecurity. In turn they find friends with similar problems, because they can relate to each other better. These mixed-up kids tend to encourage each other to do socially unacceptable things, either because it makes them feel better (drugs and alcohol) or because it brings them the attention they so badly need (even negative attention is better than none).

c. *Non-conventional Families.* These families include single parents, stepparents and "blended" families (both parents have children from another marriage). All of these are common. This topic is so complex that it will form the basis of my next book. In brief, the biggest problems the single-parent family faces involve the loss of one parent (because kids tend to love both their parents no matter what); and the lack of time and energy most single parents have to devote to their teen. A stepparent usually causes resentment because he or she is a stranger who is replacing a loved parent, and so is seen as taking away some of the natural parent's time and affection. In some blended families parents treat their own children differently than their stepchildren. All of these complications add to the teen's insecurity.

SYMPTOMS OF DEVELOPING PROBLEMS

In Chapter 1 we discussed how to recognize normal teenage behavior. This knowledge is extremely important in spotting the first signs of changes in typical behavior which could be an indication of emerging problems. Changes might include:

- new friends
- radical new hairstyle
- different clothing style
- loss of interest in activities that had been important
- more argumentative
- greater than normal need to be alone
- consistent breaking of rules
- sudden drop in school marks
- abrupt change in type of music
- sudden change in eating patterns
- insomnia or the need for unusual amounts of sleep
- persistent lying or stealing

Once again, don't panic if you see some of these signs; they may not mean major problems are developing.

THE PROBLEM-SOLVING METHOD

If your teen is acting differently or displaying any of the above symptoms, work through this method until you either discover that you don't really have a problem, or find out the cause and a way to deal with it.

1. ***Do your homework***

   If you suspect serious problems exist, it's wise to check with a professional to see if the behavior really is unusual. Teachers and school counselors are a good place to start, as they are in daily contact with the teen. See if they have noticed the same problem and if they too are worried about them. Go down to the local library and check out some books on the problem. There are a wide variety of these books available, on topics such as drug and alcohol abuse, sex, eating disorders and depression.

   Your next assignment is to examine what has been happening in the family. The changes in your teen may seem sudden, but it usually takes a while before they are noticed. Have there been unusual tensions or situations in the recent past? Has a close relative died? Is your teen's sister or brother requiring more attention right now? If such a factor can be identified, you need to take immediate steps to correct the situation.

   If an honest examination of the family shows no problems, check the peer situation. Have there been problems with friends, such as rejection from the peer group, teasing to the point of persecution or pressure to do things that your teen wouldn't normally do? To find out, you need to sit down with your teen and discuss things, calmly as usual.

2. ***Initiate a discussion***

   Pick a quiet moment when your teen is not distracted and ask if you can talk for a few minutes. This is often the hardest part of the process — getting started. Say something like "Bill, there's something I'd like to talk about. Is this a good time for you?" If you receive a "Yes," launch into the problem. If not, agree on a time, preferably on the same day, when you can talk. Next, follow these steps:

a. *Share your concern about the problem.* Tell the teen what symptoms or behavior you have observed, and why it is bothering you. Make a clear statement like "I'm very worried about your school grades. They have dropped quite a bit this term." Then ask if the teen has an explanation. **Don't react to initial defensiveness or anger.** Focus on the problem. If you notice any emotion, make a comment like "You seem frustrated," or "You seem pretty depressed about the situation." Then let the teen talk.

b. *Generate possible solutions together.* Ask the teen if he has any ideas on how to deal with this problem. Add some of your own, based on your conversation or on ideas from books or other sources. Try to examine as many solutions as possible. Don't immediately discard any of them, and do not block the conversation with a comment like "That's ridiculous" or "Don't be stupid."

c. *Come to a mutually agreeable solution.* Discuss the alternatives you have both come up with, then agree on an approach to the problem. Both parties have to be satisfied that the solution can work.

d. *Put the decision into action.* Sometimes it's helpful to write down the solution so that it's clear to both sides, and doesn't get distorted by time. In any case, begin with the agreement immediately.

This approach is useful for anything from minor problems, such as regularly failing to take out the garbage, to major concerns such as failing school grades or apparent depression. If the problem persists after making an honest effort to follow these steps, then it's out of your hands. Time to get professional help.

3. *Seek professional help*

When all your attempts at solving the problem have failed, it's time to get a mediator. **Sometimes emotions are so strong that reason and logic don't have a chance**. Getting someone neutral to help with the problem could be the answer.

To find professional help, get recommendations from someone who has experience with professionals. This might be a friend who has had a good experience, or more likely it will be a school counselor or church minister. Ask these people for their suggestions. If money is a factor, there are many state or provincial agencies that offer services for free, or on a sliding-scale basis. If these resource people do not have suggestions, look under "Counselors" or "Psychologists" in the classified ad section of the phone book. Be sure that the professional you choose is registered in your state or province as a psychologist, as these people must conform to government-set standards of training, ethics and behavior.

Many organizations offer counseling, both individual and group, for specific problems. For example, Alcoholics Anonymous offers special programs for teens who abuse alcohol, and Al-Anon is for families of alcoholics. There are agencies for drug abusers; Parents Anonymous (for parents who have lost control of their teen); and parent education programs run by the local YMCA, Red Cross, community association, or Parent-Teacher association. Again, the school counselor is a good place to start, as he or she will have pamphlets, telephone numbers, and contact people for most these organizations.

> *For parents who care, there is almost always an answer.*

For parents who care, there is almost always an answer. It will probably mean a lot of work for you. **For your teen to change, parents usually have to change first.** You can't just send the teenager off to a counselor and have him sent back cured. But you can solve the problem if you really want to.

SOME MAJOR PROBLEMS

Following are the most common problems parents of teens experience, along with suggested solutions. The common theme is STAY CALM. Whenever emotion enters the picture, it becomes distorted.

"My Teen Has the Wrong Friends"

Most parents fear the effects of a teen's friends on their child. Peer pressure can have dramatic results. Parents often are good judges of suitable friends for their teen. That's why it's so scary when it appears that your child is hanging around with the wrong group.

1. *Make sure they really are a bad influence*

   Get to know the friends by encouraging your teen to bring them home to meet you. Sometimes clothes and hairstyles can cover up some pretty nice kids. Talk to them. Find out what they like to do, how they do in school and where they live. Watch carefully for a few weeks to see if the group tends to get into trouble, either at school or in the neighborhood. At this point you may change your mind about them and relax. If not, move on to the next step.

2. *Discuss the situation with your teen*

   The emphasis here is on "discuss." Rather than issue orders like "You are not allowed to hang around with that kid," sit down with your teen and ask questions. These take the form of "Are you sure that J— is a good influence on you?" or "Do you think it's wise to hang around with J—?" If the teen asks why you want to know, explain your concerns. This takes the form of "J— doesn't seem to have a very good attitude towards school" or "J— doesn't seem to spend much time at home."

   Don't let an argument start. If the teen starts to defend the friend or argue with you, avoid debate. You have expressed your concerns and made your teen aware of the dangers of that particular friend or groups of friends. If your relationship with your teen is good, your words will have an effect. It may take a while, but if you can avoid putting them on the defensive, the chances are good that you will soon see a change. If not, the next step is in order.

3. *Seek professional help*

   If your teen and his or her friends are continually getting into trouble, and your words are obviously having no effect, you have a more serious problem than just peer group pressure. Your teen is staying with these people because he or she is getting support from them. The question becomes "Why is this support needed?" If you have followed the suggestions in the problem-solving method (see pages 190 to 192), and still can't come up with a cause, the situation is beyond your capabilities. You need to see a professional to find out what the causes really are. This is the hard part because you may not like the answers. Getting your teen to see a counselor will also be very difficult. The trick is to find a counselor who relates well to teens. You can usually get the teen to go the first time, but after that it will depend on how the counselor handled that first interview. Ask anyone who might know of a counselor who is good with teens, such as the school counselor, a minister or a Parents Anonymous chapter. Then be prepared for some hard work. As the parent, you will have to be the responsible one.

"My Teen is Smoking"

One of the great mysteries of modern society is why teens still smoke. From an early age they are exposed to all the necessary information about the dangers, yet some teens still take up the habit. Some get hooked and can't quit. The reasons aren't really much different than those of previous, less informed generations: it makes them seem more adult; it's part of the teen rebellion; they know teens don't usually get cancer; and peer pressure. One disturbing difference with this generation is that more girls than boys are taking up the habit.

If you suspect that your teen is smoking, try the following:

1. *Let them know where you stand*

   It is vital to let them know that you disapprove. Teens aren't subtle, so there are lots of clues that they are smoking. The smell, deodorizers in their room or the car, and possession of a lighter or matches all give the game away. As calmly as possible, let them know you do not approve and make it clear that you will not tolerate smoking in your home. If you smoke it is vital that you quit. A "Do as I say, not as I do" approach does not work with teens.

   The chances are that the teen is experimenting, and your intervention may be just what they need to buck peer pressure. If this fails, move on to the next step.

   > **You can't control them when they are out of your sight.**

2. *Look for more serious problems*

   There really is nothing more a parent can do than letting the teen know where you stand. You can't control them when they are out of your sight. They can lie about the smoke smell coming from being around friends who smoke. *Persistent* smoking is most often a sign of a more serious problem with self-esteem or self-image. It often goes along with having the wrong friends. Once again, follow the steps in the problem-solving section to try to find a cause and, if necessary, seek professional help.

"I Think My Teen is Using Drugs/Alcohol"

This situation is similar to smoking, but more alarming for most parents. It's common to overreact when drug or alcohol use is suspected. Here again it's important to realize that teens will experiment and will react to peer pressure. Both drugs and alcohol are readily available to those who really want them. Keeping your emotions in check in the face of this type of experimentation can seem impossible. But it is vital to do so. If you suspect your teen of using one or both of these substances, read on.

1. *Let them know you trust them*

   Teens should become educated about drugs and alcohol in school *and* at home, before they start attending parties where these things are available. Tell them they will be exposed to these substances, but you trust them to make the right decisions. Explain that they will often be tempted by good friends and occasionally even made fun of by the "users," but you know they will not give in. Keep the talk short and positive. The teen will feel good about being trusted and will try hard not to let you down.

2. *Set the example*

   As with smoking, words will carry much more weight if parents limit their own drinking. If you use liquor at all, differentiate between adult and teen drinking. The point to concentrate on is that adults know their own limits, and (excluding problem drinkers and alcoholics) drink to relax. Teens tend to drink to get drunk, and rarely have the experience to control their intake.

   In most places teens are under age and it is illegal for them to drink alcohol. Teens understand these points, especially if they don't see their parents abusing the stuff.

   Since drugs are illegal (except under medical supervision), parents should not use them at all. There are no arguments for adult usage that will hold water with a teen.

3. *Give consequences for offenses*

   Occasionally, despite all the warnings and talks, a teen will get drunk or high. Disciplinary action is immediately required. Even though you realize that experimentation is common in teens, you need not tolerate it. It is a serious offense and you want no more repetitions. The consequence should be appropriate to the circumstances and, consistent with the philosophy of this book, should be discussed with the teen first. However, a NO TOLERANCE policy should be in effect from the earliest teen years.

You must have proof that the offense has occurred. Suspicions are not enough. If the teen has a liquor breath (despite using gum, mints, even peanut butter to mask the smell), has been caught at school, or has other clear signs of inebriation, decide on the consequences with your teen. If you have only suspicions, be extra vigilant in the future, but do nothing at the time.

"I had been drinking at a party but had stopped early and already had the start of a hangover. When my parents came to pick me up they could tell I had been drinking and they got their little revenge and their point across. When we got home they turned on the vacuum, played loud music with drums and kept yelling in my ear. I wasn't allowed to sleep for a while, and I haven't got drunk after that." - Sabrina

4. *If the problem persists*
   There is no doubt that drinking or using drugs on a regular basis goes far beyond "experimenting." If the suggested steps have not worked and you know for certain that your teen is abusing a substance, repeat the problem-solving method. If you can't find the causes or are unable to solve the problems, *get professional help.* There are many agencies, both private and government funded, to turn to for help. Again, avoid panicking. Be prepared for some hard work. And be patient.

"How Do I Get My Teen to Do Homework?"

It should be no surprise that good grades are often far more important to parents than to teens. Parents know that academic performance which qualifies for post-secondary education is a major component of securing a good job. Teens "know" this, but really can't see far enough into the future to be concerned.

Completing homework accomplishes two things. It proves that the teen cares about school, and it helps in getting good grades. If you notice that little homework is being done, or if you are getting frequent notifications from school that assignments are not complete, follow this sequence of steps:

1. *Make sure you know your teen's ability level*

   While your teen's academic ability is not directly related to doing homework, it does affect grades. What you need to know is whether your teen is working at the level of his or her ability and getting appropriate grades.

   By the time your teenager reaches junior high, you should know what his or her academic capabilities are. Grades, teacher comments and standardized testing results are all available to help you to determine this objectively. You can't judge your child's ability level by what you or your spouse did in school. You have to honestly hear what the teacher is saying, then set your standards accordingly.

   Once this is done, keep in touch with your child's school performance to see that it reflects his or her true abilities. As long as it does, *don't worry about homework too much*. Of course everyone can always do better, but pushing too hard can be as bad as not caring at all. If the gap between ability and performance starts to increase, then you'll need to go to the next step.

2. *Help them become organized*

   In order to finish homework, students needs to be organized. They will need:

   a. a place to work undisturbed (the teen's own room is best, the kitchen or family room the worst);

   b. a desk, a good desk lamp, a supply of pens, pencils and paper;

   c. a planner or homework notebook to note daily assignments, and a calendar with large squares (to write in) above or near the desk to keep track of long-term assignments;

   d. a separate notebook for each subject; and

e.   a backpack or book bag to carry everything back and
forth.

The next step is to help them develop a series of habits. These
include:

a.   keeping track of the assignments in their homework notebook (you may have to check this for a while);

b.   checking their homework book to ensure all books needed
for the night's session have been taken home;

c.   starting homework at the same time each night (this may
have to be modified slightly to allow for lessons and practices; in this case set up a schedule for each day);

d.   putting all books and notes together at the end of the session, and placing the book bag where it won't be forgotten
the next day.

Hint: I usually recommend the time between school and supper not be used for homework, but as a wind-down period.

Start these habits early in junior high so that they are well
entrenched by high school. For the first two or three months
gentle reminders may be necessary, so some checking up is
necessary. If this proves to be insufficient, stronger actions may
be required.

3.   *When the school starts calling*
Most schools have caring teachers who will call you when major assignments are not done, or when marks are at the failing
level. Whether you discover a problem through these calls or
through report cards, it's time to get serious.

Set up a monitoring system with the school that informs
you on a daily basis what homework the student has. This
type of system (such as a daybook that has to be signed by
every class teacher each day) requires considerable time and
energy on your part. First, you must check the book before
homework starts to see what has to be done. Next, the homework is checked for completeness at the end, and then you
sign the book.

This system will break down if the student "forgets" to get the book signed by teachers. Disorganized students do tend to forget, while unmotivated ones just don't bother. If forgetting becomes a habit, take away a privilege, or add chores as a consequence.

The system also doesn't work if parents don't keep up their end. Consistency on everyone's part is vital. Keep this up for two weeks to a month (few parents have the energy to monitor this closely any longer), then let the teen go solo. Those who truly want to do better will improve.

4. *Nothing is working*

   If you have tried all these steps and your teen's performance is still nowhere near potential, a message is being given. The teen is rebelling against parental authority; the self-esteem is so low that the teen does not believe in his or her ability; or, there are other personal problems. Most teens want to do well in school, and are upset when they don't. If you don't see signs of concern and subsequent improvement, use the problem-solving method and/or seek professional help from a counselor or therapist.

"My Teenager is Always on the Telephone"

It bothers most parents to see their teen spending a lot of time on the telephone. This may relate to a feeling that time should be spent achieving a goal rather than in apparently aimless conversation. The reality is, teens really believe that they cannot live without Bell's best-known invention. Phone lines are their link to the friends that are so important to them. Realizing this, some compromises need to be made between the parents' attitude that teens should be doing something useful, and the kids' approach that the telephone comes first.

1. *Assess how big a problem you have*

   The first step is to determine whether or not you really have a problem. Are homework and chores not being done because of gabbing? Is the teen's use of the phone interfering with household life in any way? This would certainly be true if mom is in real estate and can't get her calls through because daughter is on the line. If you don't have a problem, why worry? Save your concern for major issues.

By the way, teenage girls need a phone much more often than most of their male peers, at least during the earlier teen years.

2. *If there's a battle for the phone*

When parents rely on the telephone for their own purposes, or when there are several teens in the same household, limits may need to be set on phone time. If you can, get call waiting, or better still, a separate teen line. Have them pay at least part of the cost out of their allowance so they appreciate that this is a considerable expense.

If this technological solution works, great. If there are still hassles, then limits must be set on talk time. Be aware that this requires monitoring, which in turn requires time, energy and peacemaking skills. If you have a teenager you already know their sense of time is not well-developed. You will have to intervene occasionally to remind them that their time is up and it's little sister's turn.

Call a family meeting to set guidelines, such as who has what time slot, and how much time each teen is allotted in one turn. Consistent abuse of the guidelines will require penalties, usually in the form of withdrawal of telephone privileges.

3. *Homework and/or chores are not getting done*

Homework and chores should always come before the telephone. As mentioned, homework should be done at a set time each night. Chores can also be organized to be done at regular times. If telephone calls are interfering with any of these tasks, then no calls should be allowed. Friends quickly learn that Sally isn't allowed calls between 7:00 and 8:00 each night and will generally respect these limits. If Billy doesn't know these rules, and calls during this time, then parents should politely ask him to call back after 8:00. Some parents get so caught up in this

A TELEPHONE TALE

I have two children, now at the end of their teenage journey. Though they are different in nature, throughout their teen years the only thing that caused friction between them was the telephone.

My son, the oldest, required the phone infrequently at first. One line was sufficient. Once my daughter hit puberty, circumstances changed radically. My wife and I then installed another line. All went well for a couple of years until my son added a modem to the family computer. He then tied up the teen line for hours on end, talking to people on screen that he could have talked to more easily on the telephone. Friction between brother and sister started again. To end this controversy, we had call waiting added to their line.

This proved to be nothing but an aggravation. The call waiting tone electronically interfered with the modem, ending the session and causing howls of anguish from my son. Fortunately, after many calls to the telephone company, we found a solution.

For a short period of time all went well, until my son acquired a girlfriend in another city. Since his calls to or from her were long distance, he didn't want to pay for any more time than he had to. He wouldn't answer call waiting while talking to her. More screams from my daughter — and rightly so. Rules had to be made to cover this circumstance.

Along the way we had lengthy discussions about things like teen friends calling our line when the "hot line" was busy; son spending too much time on the modem; and daughter purposely picking up the line to scramble the modem and cause garbage on the screen. There never seemed to be a solution that would cover all contingencies. If you find one that works for everything, congratulations and please send it to me for future reference.

telephone problem that they tend to be rude to the friends that they think are abusing the system. This embarrasses the teen and often leads to battles.

If the teen has her own line and receives the calls directly, she can simply tell the friend she will call them back. The difficulty comes when the call has to do with mutual homework. This is a legitimate reason to take or make a call during the banned period, but the conversation often drifts to other topics. Your guideline should be — if the homework is getting done, don't worry about it. If problems start, then monitor the calls more closely, and assess penalties if the teen is persistent. Be calm and consistent when applying these consequences — don't rush into the room and rip out the phone. It's hard on the equipment, and it causes hurt feelings.

Again, all rules should be agreed upon by all parties, either at a family meeting or in one-on-one sessions with a parent. Be prepared for exceptions, poor memories, and bad timekeeping. But you will never eliminate all the problems with this evil instrument.

"What About Teens and Sex?"

This is a very scary area for most parents. You hear lots of stories and statistics about how sexually active teens are, but unless you are in close communication with your teen, you have no way of knowing how much of it is true. There is also a flood of data about sexually-transmitted diseases, including the dreaded AIDS, that is even more worrisome. One revealing statistic is that only about 40 percent of parents talk to their teens about sex. This is the place to start.

1. *Give your teen as much accurate information as possible about sexuality*
   Some school systems actively teach sex education, and others don't. In either case, it is not safe to *assume* anything about how much your teen knows. I have been a resource person for a sex-education unit and found students holding many

misconceptions. The best approach is to sit down with your teen and discuss the subject in as much detail as possible. Use natural openings, such as after seeing a TV program or a movie where teenage pregnancy or teenage promiscuity was the theme. Don't dodge controversial issues such as homosexuality or oral sex if the teen asks. Take a deep breath and calmly discuss your ideas and opinions.

If you find that you just can't talk about these things, check out books from the library or buy them at the bookstore, wait for an opening, then ask the teen to read up on the subject. Read the book yourself in case the teen wants to ask any questions. Invite questions, then answer them factually. Answering questions can be far easier than initiating a discussion.

Prepare the teen for potentially dangerous situations. How should she handle pressure from her boyfriend to have sex? What if she's the only virgin in the crowd? Or he is? How does he handle situations where alcohol is involved? Try to get the teen to generate different scenarios, then discuss ways of dealing with them. Forewarned is forearmed.

2. *Let the teen know what your values are regarding sexual behavior*

Accurate information is important, but the values associated with that information are equally vital. Use the natural openings mentioned to open a discussion about what you feel are the rights and wrongs about sex. How do you feel about premarital sex? Is it OK as long as the teen uses a condom? Should it be restricted just to those the teen is truly in love with? Should it happen at all? What should the teen do if it does happen? If you can rationally let the teen know how you feel about the moral side of sex, and listen to how the teen feels in return, the teen will often take your values to heart. The key is to be able to discuss these issues without emotion. If you won't talk about sex, or if you react emotionally when it's mentioned, the teen will not discuss it with you.

3. *Keep your cool*

This advice has been given throughout the book, but it is even more important in a sensitive area like sex. What do you do if you find condoms in your son's room while tidying up? You certainly don't fling them at him at the supper table and demand an explanation. At an appropriate moment, discuss your find. Expect an angry accusation of invasion of privacy (hopefully, the discovery was an accident, not the result of a planned search). Keep your cool, then try to discuss his sexual activity. It's possible that he has them to feel "cool" or be one of the boys. If he is sexually active, tell him honestly how you feel about the situation. Your feeling will probably be different for a 14-year-old than an 18- or 19-year-old.

Here's a case history showing how one set of parents successfully handled this type of crisis:

Sharon was the star player on her junior high basketball team. She was attractive, and an excellent student. Her friends formed the "in" crowd of the school, with their social lives often being their main focus.

With the help of alcohol, one of their parties went from innocent card playing to a strip poker game. At the end of the game, now in the nude, Sharon was feeling woozy from the effects of the booze and went into one of the bedrooms to sleep it off. A few minutes later in came Pat, one of the most popular boys in the school, and one who Sharon had had a crush on for a long time. He lay down on the bed with her and one thing led to another until the inevitable occurred, they had sex.

On the following Monday, Sharon came to see me. The sex had been her first time, and she was feeling guilty and confused. She had an excellent relationship with her parents and wanted to discuss the situation with them, but was afraid of their reaction. I told her that I could help her prepare the way, but that she would have to do the work. After she left the office, I called Sharon's mother and told them that Sharon had something very difficult to talk over with them and that I hoped that they could hear her out and be sympathetic.

They handled it beautifully. The parents took her out for dinner, then mentioned that they understood that she needed to talk with them. Sharon could see that they were concerned so she proceeded to tell the entire story. The parents listened sympathetically, told her that they were disappointed that she had allowed herself to get into this type of situation, then discussed how she could avoid similar situations in the future.

The result was a closer than ever relationship with her parents, plus new confidence that she would not allow this type of situation to reoccur.

This is NOT a typical situation so don't panic. But it is an example of a crisis situation that you may be called upon to handle. The parents stayed calm and supportive, and were able to keep a discussion going despite their shock and disappointment. Since you won't always get a warning from the counselor that a shock is coming, it's important to prepare yourself mentally in case you're suddenly presented with a bombshell. Use the problem-solving approach whenever possible, to work out a solution.

"My Teen Might Be Considering Suicide"

This is a highly complex issue, and really deserves a more thorough treatment than this book can give it. There is little doubt that the incidence of teen suicide has been rising for a number of years. While it is still a relatively rare event, it is of concern to many parents.

1. *What are the symptoms of a suicidal teen?*

   While there are exceptions, most suicidal teens give some indications of their intentions, either through things that they say, or through their actions. Direct statements like "I wish I were dead" or "Sometimes I just want to die" should always be taken seriously. Often the words are more subtle such as "You won't have me to worry about much longer" or "I'm nothing but a problem to everyone." Whether direct or subtle, these kinds of statements are danger signs of a teen in trouble.

   Suicidal behaviors usually involve withdrawal and signs of depression. Crying jags, longer than usual periods in the room, preoccupation with darkness or questions about death and dying, and withdrawal from friends are all indications of possible suicidal thoughts.

   If any of these signs are noticed, take immediate action.

2. *Confront the problem*

   Whether the symptomatic behavior really indicates suicidal intentions or whether it is simply an attention-seeking device, a problem exists and you need to deal with it. As soon as you notice any of the behaviors listed under "symptoms", or any other worrying behavior, sit down with your teen and share your concerns. Tell her you are worried and what it is you are worried about. **Ask straight out if she is considering suicide.** Many people tiptoe around this problem in the mistaken belief that if they talk about it, they might give the teen ideas. No way. Confront the issue directly, then slide into the problem-solving method to try to find solutions. Encourage the teen to express his feelings, then concentrate on the reason behind them. *Do not* make statements like "Oh, don't be silly." Do not try to deny these feelings. If they exist, you need to deal with them, whether or not the causes really exist or are actually all that bad.

3. *Remove potentially dangerous items*

   While you are working on the causes of the problems, remove

all pills, medicines or potentially dangerous chemicals from the house. If you own firearms, ensure that they are locked up and there is no ammunition available. You can't eliminate every possibility; if the teen is serious enough, she or he can always find a way. Just try not to make it easy for them while you are working on the problem.

4. *If the symptoms persist, get professional help*
    There are depressions not related to a person's environment, but which are the result of imbalances in brain chemistry. If there is no immediate solution to your problem-solving discussions, *get help from a professional.* There are medications that can be extremely useful in combating these chemical depressions.

> *Emotions have to be kept out of confrontational situations. Stay calm, get all the facts, then look for a solution.*

These are the biggest problems many parents encounter. It can never be emphasized enough that emotions have to be kept out of confrontational situations. Stay calm, get all the facts, then look for a solution. Don't look for someone to blame — this won't help the situation. Keep communications with your teen open. If you cannot discuss problems with them, you will never be able to solve them.

Finally, keep following the "Hear Me, Hug Me, Trust Me" approach. It works.

Further Reading

This book is intended to provide a comprehensive approach to raising an adolescent, and hopefully answers most of the questions and problems that parents might have. The infinite variety of human personalities, however, makes it impossible for any one book to cover all possible topics and to answer all possible questions. As much as I'd like to believe this book does, I know better. If you have concerns that are either not mentioned in this text or are only briefly covered, then perhaps one of the books described below will be of more help.

To help you choose which book might be best for your particular situation, I've included notes about most of them. Titles alone don't always describe their contents.

I've roughly categorized the following titles by topic, rather than by the more usual approach of just listing them in alphabetical order. This list is by no means complete, but it does include most of the popular books that are readily available.

THE CLASSICS

Ginott, Haim. *Between Parent and Teenager.* New York: Macmillan, 1969.
Ginott is the originator of the gentle, non-judgmental approach to communicating with teens that he calls "The Healing Dialogue." This approach treats teens as young adults, rather than as bigger kids, and has been expanded and enlarged by many subsequent authors. The book has an excellent sec-

tion on typical teenage behavior — how they act and what they hate. It does not attempt to be a complete guide to raising teens as it leaps from communication technique to sex to driving and drugs, but it does cover many important areas. The frequent use of case histories, many now somewhat dated, makes it a highly readable, if slightly obsolete, book.

Gordon, Thomas. *Parent Effectiveness Training.* **New York: Peter H. Wyden, Inc, 1970.**
While not specifically aimed at teens, the techniques advocated in this book work as well with them as they do with younger children. Gordon does not admit it, but he uses a similar approach to communicating with teens as does Ginott. This approach has been made into a more complete system encompassing communication, discipline and conflict resolution. He is the originator of both the "I-statements" and the concept of "ownership" of problems. Both these ideas have been copied by others, often without acknowledging the source.

Gordon's "active listening" system is somewhat complex to follow by just reading the book, which is probably why it has been turned into an eight-week course offered all over North America. He is not a believer in consequences and punishments, which may be the reason the system is often considered to be permissive. If a parent has the time and interest, this book is well worth working through.

UNDERSTANDING TEENS

These are books which concentrate on finding out what the typical teen is like, and why they are like this. They are very useful for parents who are puzzled by their teen's behavior, but aren't having any serious problems.

Bradley, Michael J. *Yes, Your Teen is Crazy: Loving Your Kid without Losing Your Mind.* **Gig Harbor, WA: Harbor Press, 2002.**
This is a very well laid out book that dispenses sound advice to parents of young teenagers. It is easy to read and has a wide variety of illustrative anecdotes that really help make the points clear and understandable.

Craig, Judi. *You're Grounded Til You're Thirty: What Works and What Doesn't in Parenting Teens Today.* **New York, NY: Hearst Books, 1996.**

Also good for parents having only minor problems with their teenagers. It is a clear, easy to read, common-sense approach to understanding teenage behavior.

Empfield, Maureen & Bakalar, Nicholas. *Understanding Teenage Depression: A Guide to Diagnosis, Treatment and Management.* **New York, NY: Henry Holt & Co., 2001.**

This is a "must-read" for parents whose teenagers are subject to frequent depression. It is a thorough and detailed look at the subject which sometimes becomes heavy reading. Besides explaining the origins of depression it also gives a detailed overview of treatments available, including both psychotherapeutic and anti-depressant medication. This book also describes such other teenage problems as smoking, ADHD, eating disorders and self-mutilation. However, it tends to just describe these concerns rather than discussing treatment approaches to them.

Giannetti, Charlene, & Sagarese, Margaret. *The Roller-Coaster Years: Raising Your Child Through the Maddening Yet Magical Middle School Years.* **New York, NY: Broadway Books, 1997.**

For parents who hate jargon and tedious prose, this book will be a breath of fresh air. It not only provides a thorough understanding of the ten to fifteen year old, it gives clear advice on what to do with the problems that are encountered during these years. It is well-organized and detailed enough for parents to be able to apply the solutions that are recommended. This text is mainly for parents of pre-teens who are not yet experiencing any problems.

Langlois, Christine (Ed.). *Understanding Your Teen.* **Mississauga, ON: Ballantine Books, 1999.**

This book was created by a project team from the *Canadian Living* Magazine. It lists eight writers and a team of expert advisors who have contributed to the book's creation. As may be expected from a team approach, it is somewhat hard to follow at times, as the topic sequence tends to jump around. It is also superficial in its discussion of topics. The section entitled "When Your Teen is in Crisis" is particularly devoid of steps to follow for parents to regain control of their teenagers. However, the book is easy to read and has many useful quotes and illustrations for parents who want to know more about what makes teenagers tick.

Marshall, Peter. *Now I Know Why Tigers Eat Their Young: Surviving a New Generation of Teenagers.* **Vancouver/Toronto: Whitecap Books, 2000.**

This best-seller has been recently updated and is basically an "understanding" book that also looks at different parenting styles and their effectiveness. It is light and humorous, with an excellent chapter on the consultation/negotiating process. The text is relatively short, but the major points can sometimes be hard to pick out in the text. This is a good book for parents of relatively average teenagers as it is full of good tips on how to handle them.

Vedral, Joyce. *My Teenager is Driving Me Crazy.* **New York: Ballantine Books, 1989.**

An excellent book for understanding teens. It uses a similar approach to my book as the author has solicited teen quotes to support her points. (This was a bit disappointing to me, I thought I had an original idea but Vedral beat me to it.) The author covers most of the troublesome areas of teen behavior, giving clear insights into how teens think. The book is a little short of concrete suggestions, but well worth reading for an understanding of how and why teens do what they do.

Wolf, Anthony. *Get Out of My Life, but First Could You Drive Me and Cheryl to the Mall.* **New York, NY: Farrar, Straus & Giroux, 2002.**

The title to this recently re-issued book gives a clear indication that it is a light and humorous approach to understanding teens. It is easy to read, yet provides great insights into the mind of today's teenager. While it is not a complete parenting system, it does provide good advice on communication, handling conflict and many other problems that parents are liable to encounter while raising their teens. This is highly recommended for parents who are vexed by their teens' behavior but are not yet experiencing serious problems.

PARENTING SYSTEMS

This section includes books, like this one, that try to give an overall approach to the parenting of teens. They are aimed at parents of young teens and even pre-adolescents so that major problems are avoided in later years.

Bluestein, Jane. *Parents, Teens and Boundaries: How to Draw the Line.* Deerfield Beach, FL: Health Communications Inc., 1993.

Including exercises in a book like this is an interesting approach, but tends to put many parents off. In this case, it would be wise to buy this book, even if you ignore the exercises. It is a sound approach to setting boundaries, which is something that many modern parents really need.

Bluestein includes more than just boundary-setting, she also outlines the essential ingredients for developing sound relationships with teenagers including love, respect, acceptance and communication. This is a very useful book, especially for parents of young teenagers.

Dinkmeyer, Don and Gary McKay. *Parenting Teenagers.* Circle Pines, MN: American Guidance Service, 1990.

This is a reprint of a 1983 work called *The Parent's Guide*. It is a "workbook" approach, based on a program called "Sytematic Training for Effective Parenting," which includes exercises to do at home. It devotes three chapters to understanding teens, and also has a good section on building self-esteem. The communication chapter is built on Dr. Thomas Gordon's *Parent Effectiveness Training*, but simplifies the approach for easier understanding. From communication it moves on to two chapters on discipline, under which the authors have included a section on developing responsibility.

This is a very thorough approach which includes many cartoons for clarification. It often gets to be very heavy reading, such as the section on "How to Phrase a Reflective Listening Response," but is excellent for the parent who has the time and energy to follow through with this approach. It definitely would work best as the text for the S.T.E.P. course.

Phelan, Thomas. *Surviving Your Adolescents: How to Manage and Let Go of Your 13-18 Year Olds.* **Glen Ellyn, IL: Child Management Inc., 1998.**

Phelan is the author of the very excellent "1-2-3 Magic" program for younger children. His book for parents of teenagers is brief and somewhat superficial, but has many excellent insights for parents baffled by their teenagers' behavior. The "four cardinal sins" of parents section is particularly enlightening, and there is some very good advice given on communication techniques.

Popkin, Michael. *Active Parenting of Teens.* **Atlanta: Active Parenting, Inc., 1990.**

This is also a "workbook" approach, used with a parent education program called Active Parenting. The main philosophy is that by being active in parenting, you avoid being reactive to problems at a later date. It also relies heavily on the *Parent Effectiveness Training* of Dr. Thomas Gordon, and credits him for his ideas. The book spends only a brief amount of time on understanding, and moves quickly into the areas of building self-esteem, solving problems, and communication techniques. There is also a very good chapter on how to hold family meetings.

This is a very useful book for parents of young teens. It includes exercises, has excellent summaries, and the problem-solving technique is superb. It is hard work, but well worth the effort.

Windell, James. *6 Steps to an Emotionally Intelligent Teenager.* **New York, NY: John Wiley & Sons, 1999.**

While this book involves a lot of work for parents, the work will pay huge dividends in developing stable, emotionally healthy individuals. Throughout the book, Windell displays a thorough understanding of what teenagers need and want. He begins with a chapter on how to go about teaching the skills he believes teenagers need, then launches into his six-step approach. These steps include:

1) Teach Your Teen to Set Goals

2) Teach Your Teen to Identify and Change Self-defeating Behaviors

3) Teach Your Teen to be Assertive

4) Teach Your Teenager to Have Feelings for Others

5) Teach Your Teenager to Handle Anger

6) Teach Your Teenager to Resolve Conflicts Peacefully.

There is also a section on "Parenting the Difficult Teen" which, along with the section on handling anger, will be most useful to parents who are already experiencing difficulties with their teenagers.

COMMUNICATION

Faber, Adele and Elaine Mazlish. *How to Talk So Kids Will Listen & Listen So Kids Will Talk.* **New York: Avon Books, 1999.**

This book is not specifically designed for communication with teens, but the techniques will work well. While the title was borrowed from two of Dr. Thomas Gordon's chapter headings, the overall system is simpler. Besides the four-step communication system, the book also discusses the areas of responsibility (gaining cooperation), discipline (alternatives to punishment) and freedom (developing autonomy). It also has a problem-solving method which can be extremely effective with teens.

Overall, it is very easy to read, provides lots of summaries and illustrative cartoons, and some exercises to practice. A highly-recommended book.

Heyman, Richard. *How to Say It to Teens: Talking About the Most Important Topics of Their Lives.* **Paramus, NJ: Prentice Hall Press, 2001.**

This is an especially useful book for parents of young teenagers as it gives very clear guidelines on how to talk about eighty-eight different topics that parents usually find very difficult. The book starts with five basic communication principles that will be helpful in discussing any topic with teenagers. Then, for each of the topics there are sections on Things to Consider, Three Things You Must Do, What to Say & Do and What Not to Say and Do.

TROUBLESHOOTING GUIDES

These are books that are specifically designed to help parents who are experiencing problems with their teenager. They cover everything from minor, everyday teen conflicts to major issues such as drugs and suicide.

Bayard, Robert and Jean. *How to Deal With Your Acting-Up Teenager.* **Markham, Ont: Fitzhenry & Whiteside, 1998.**
This book outlines a comprehensive program to follow when you have lost control of your teen. The approach is based heavily on Dr. Thomas Gordon's P.E.T system, but geared specifically to serious problems. It involves teaching the teens responsibility for their lives, learning to trust the teen's decisions, and changing your ideas about the teen. It is hard work, but the book is excellent for dealing with serious problems such as chronic lying, stealing and refusing to obey house rules. This is probably the best book available for parents of out-of-control teenagers.

Bernstein, Neil. *How to Keep Your Teenager Out of Trouble and What to Do if You Can't.* **New York, NY: Workman Publishing Co., 2001.**
This book begins with an excellent chapter on how teenagers get into trouble, then launches into ways of preventing and dealing with teenage behavior problems. It is a clearly-written guide that is easy for parents to follow and is comprehensive in its scope. This book will be effective both for parents of teens who are just beginning to get into trouble and for those who are already out-of-control. Highly recommended.

Elkind, David. *Parenting Your Teenager in the 90's.* **Rosemont, NJ: Modern Learning Press, 1993.**
Elkind is generally considered to be one of the foremost experts on parenting in North America. This book is a collection of his monthly columns from *Parents Magazine* over a period of five years. It is divided into sections dealing with emotional and psychological development, friendship and dating, family matters, education, and adapting to society. It covers a wide range of topics from teen anxiety to homosexuality. The book is written

in a very readable style, with the solutions to the problems clearly laid out. It not only provides insight into how teens think and feel, but it is a superb reference book to have on the shelf in case problems, major or minor, do arise.

Fleming, Don. *How to Stop the Battle with Your Teenager: A Practical Guide for Solving Everyday Problems.* **New York, NY: Simon and Schuster, 1993.**

This is a specific problem-solving guide to most common teenage problems, which features a carefully laid out step-by-step approach to solving each problem. For example, the author details four distinct steps to take if the teen tends to leave personal items around the house. The book includes an excellent chapter on discipline, and another good one on "anti-social behavior," but only briefly touches on communication. It is probably best for minor problems, as it does not outline an overall problem-solving approach. Instead it gives individual, 4-step solutions to a wide variety of difficulties.

Pipher, Mary. *Reviving Ophelia: Saving the Selves of Adolescent Girls.* **New York, NY: Ballantine Books, 1994.**

While this book is often very heavy reading, it thoroughly discusses most of the problems that are either unique to or more prevalent in teenage girls such as weight, sex and depression. It uses detailed case histories to illustrate the main points. These are excellent insights from a very experienced therapist.

Sells, Scott. *Parenting Your Out-of-Control Teenager.* **New York, NY: St. Martin's Griffin, 2001.**

This book includes an excellent section on how parents lose control in the first place, which provides the rational for the rest of the text. The book is worth it for this section alone as, if you know what you did wrong, you are already half way to fixing the problems. Sells provides step-by-step solutions to these problems that parents can easily follow. Many are done with considerable humor, which may be too bizarre for some parents, but most parents will find effective strategies for their particular difficulties.

BOOKS FOR TEENAGERS

If you have a teen that likes to read, and you are having normal teen-type problems such as messy rooms, arguments, or failure to do chores, you might want to try what psychologists call bibliotherapy (book cures). The following books are written for teens to understand their parents. The first is written in dictionary form for quick reference, and is fairly serious, but the other two are light and easy to read. They might help your teen to see things from the other side, and not get so worked up in disputes.

Johnson, Eric. *How to Live with Parents and Teachers*. Philadelphia: The Westminster Press, 1986.

Packer, Alex. *Bringing Up Parents*. Washington, DC: Acropolis Books, 1985. (Comes with a money-back guarantee — honest)

Vedral, Joyce. *My Parents Are Driving Me Crazy*. New York: Ballantine Books, 1986.

INDEX

SUGGESTIONS & COMMENTS

_____

_____

_____

_____

_____

_____

_____

_____

_____

_____

_____

_____

_____

_____

_____

_____

_____

_____